CETSHWAYO'S DUTCHMAN

CETSHWAYO
(From a Photograph by J.E. Bruton)

Cetshwayo's Dutchman

Being the Private Journal of a White Trader in Zululand During the British Invasion

Cornelius Vijn

Translated and Edited by
the Right Rev. J. W. Colenso, D.D.,
Bishop of Natal

Greenhill Books

This edition of *Cetshwayo's Dutchman* first published 1988
by Greenhill Books, Lionel Leventhal Limited,
1 Russell Gardens, London NW11 9NN.

Distributed in the United States by
Presidio Press,
31 Pamaron Way, Novato, CA. 94947.

British Library Cataloguing in Publication Data
Vijn, Cornelius
Cetshwayo's Dutchman: Being the Private Journal of a White Trader
in Zululand during the British Invasion.
1. Zulu War
I. Title   II. Colenso, J.W. (John William), *d.1883*   968.4'045

ISBN 1-85367-007-3

Publishing History
Cetshwayo's Dutchman was first published in 1880
(Longmans, Green & Co.). This edition presents the text of the
original volume, with the addition of illustrations from
The Illustrated London News and *The Graphic*.
The Publishers wish to express their thanks to Mr. John Young
in making available these illustrations.
The text in the original, rare volume is fragile and this creates
imperfections when reproduced and which necessarily appear in
this facsimile volume.

Printed by Antony Rowe Limited,
Chippenham, Wiltshire.

CONTENTS

PAGE

THE PRIVATE JOURNAL OF CETSHWAYO'S DUTCHMAN.........1

NOTES BY THE BISHOP OF NATAL..83

APPENDIX

THE ZULU MILITARY SYSTEM..189

A PROTEST AGAINST THE ZULU WAR 193

LIST OF ILLUSTRATIONS

From the John Young Collection

1. Cetshwayo (*The Graphic*)

2. Cetshwayo in captivity, the Castle, Cape Town. (*The Graphic*)

3. Peace negotiations at Nonchasini, June 1879. (*The Graphic*)

4. Cetshwayo, the Zulu King. "Drawn from the life in June, 1877, by the late Mr. Edward Tilt, during his visit to Zululand." (*Illustrated London News*)

5. Dabulamanzi, brother of King Cetshwayo, Commander of the Zulu Army at Isandhlwana. (*Illustrated London News*)

6. Vijn's letter being handed to Lord Chelmsford, accompanying the return by Cetshwayo of the Prince Imperial's Sword. (*Illustrated London News*)

7. The last battle at Ulundi. On the left are Cetshwayo's renegade brothers' warriors in combat with a Cetshwayo warrior. The illustration of the costume worn is surprisingly accurate. (*The Graphic*)

8. The surrender at Ulundi, 1st September 1879. Third from the right is Sir Garnet Wolseley and guiding Gaozi's hand is Mr. T. Shepstone, the interpreter. (*The Graphic*)

1. Cetshwayo (*The Graphic*)

2. Cetshwayo in captivity, the Castle, Cape Town. (*The Graphic*)

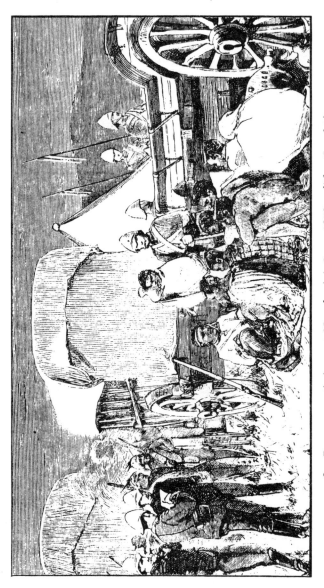

3. Peace negotiations at Nonchasini, June 1879. (*The Graphic*)

4. Cetshwayo, the Zulu King. "Drawn from the life in June, 1877, by the late Mr. Edward Tilt, during his visit to Zulu-land." (*Illustrated London News*)

5. Dabulamanzi, brother of King Cetshwayo,
Commander of the Zulu Army at Isandhlwana.
(*Illustrated London News*)

6. Vijn's letter being handed to Lord Chelmsford, accompanying the return by Cetshwayo of the Prince Imperial's Sword. (*Illustrated London News*)

7. The last battle at Ulundi. On the left are Cetshwayo's renegade brothers' warriors in combat with a Cetshwayo warrior. The illustration of the costume worn is surprisingly accurate. (*The Graphic*)

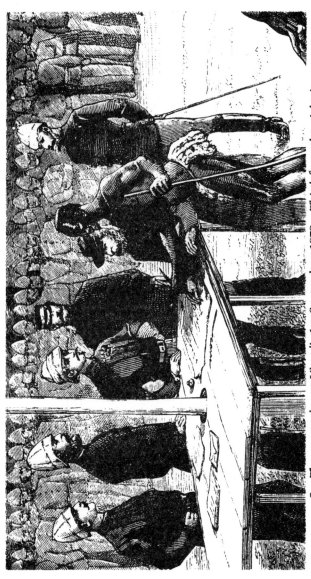

8. The surrender at Ulundi, 1st September 1879. Third from the right is Sir Garnet Wolseley and guiding Gaozi's hand is Mr. T. Shepstone, the interpreter. (*The Graphic*)

PREFACE.

Mr. Cornelius Vijn is a young Hollander, 23 years old, who has been 4½ years in Natal, during three-fourths of which time (as he states) he has been trading in Zululand, and has thus learned to speak the Zulu language well, though he would not undertake to write it, and has become thoroughly conversant with the Zulu people, and their ordinary habits and customs. He was educated at the Town Burgher-School of Hoorn, in Holland, and, of course, speaks and writes European Dutch, in which language the narrative of his sojourn in Zululand during the late war was written by him. But since his arrival in Natal he has learned to speak freely in the English tongue—very well indeed for a foreigner—though, as his letters printed in the ' Notes ' will show, he does not write English quite grammatically. On the whole, however, he is a young man of fair education and good intelligence; and his character is such, on the authority of an English Colonist who knows him well, as to warrant entire confidence being placed in his statements as to what he has heard, or seen, or known, in Zululand.

Mr. Vijn has placed his manuscript in my hands with the request that I would cast my eye over it, and say whether it would be worth while to publish it in England, at the present crisis of Zulu affairs. Having perused it I found that it was well worthy of being published and made accessible to English readers. And I have accordingly undertaken to translate it, and supply a series of Notes,[1] which may throw further light on the matters referred to in it, and especially on the character and conduct of Cetshwayo.[2]

---

[1] Some of the information in the Notes has been obtained by my head-printer ' Magema,' who, under authority from Sir G. Wolseley, was sent, in October, 1879, into Zululand to recover, if possible, the watch, or other relics, of the late Prince Imperial, and ascertain the manner of his death (Note 46).

[2] In this name C represents a click; but, if the English readers pronounce the name as ' Ketsh-wa-yo ' (*a* sounded as in

My own very strong conviction is that the Zulu King has been grossly misrepresented by those who have wished to find some support in his doings for waging, in the name and with the power of Christian England, the late most unjust and wicked war —a war which at first was said to be waged against the King, and not against the Zulu Nation, a figment which was afterwards abandoned by Lord Chelmsford, who says that, though 'at its first commencement such an announcement, that our quarrel was with Cetshwayo alone, was politic and proper, as it afforded an opportunity to those Chiefs who were averse to Cetshwayo's rule to come over to our side' [2318, p. 56], yet 'it is clear that the Zulu People themselves are not prepared to accept the distinction it was thought desirable to make' [*Ib.* p. 81], and which Sir G. Wolseley, in the face of the plain facts, has again revived.

In particular Sir B. Frere has been unceasing in his efforts to blacken Cetshwayo's character and to make him appear odious in the eyes of Englishmen,

'father '), they will come near enough to the native pronounciation for all practical purposes. It is quite wrong to spell and pronounce it as a word of *four* syllables, *e.g.* 'Ce-te-wa-yo.'

who would never have endured, as they have done hitherto—very reluctantly, it is true, and with grave misgivings—that such things should have been done in their name in these parts, if they had not been led to suppose that the Zulu King was really the loathsome monster which Sir B. Frere has persistently represented him to be. Indeed when we read the touching account of the devotion of the Zulu People to their King in his hour of utmost need (Note 32), and of their respect for him even after his fall,[1]—of

---

[1] Mr. Cross is reported to have said at Leigh (*Guardian*, Oct. 15, 1879):—' Of the result of the Zulu War I may safely say this—because I have personally conversed with a great number of persons who have come from that country—that, if anybody is glad at that result, it is the people of Zululand themselves, who have escaped from the tyranny to which they were subjected.' It is difficult to see who the '*great number of persons who have come from that country* (Zululand),' and with whom Mr. Cross has 'personally conversed,' can have been. He can hardly have meant military persons, who almost all left Natal before the capture of Cetshwayo, and could have known nothing of the feeling of the Zulu People towards their King, except very superficially, and then through an interpreter. And I doubt much if any single person who has resided in Zululand— *e.g.* Trader or Missionary—has visited England since the capture of the King or even since the beginning of the war, except Mr. John Mullins, who would not, I imagine, support Mr. Cross's statement, which is contradicted by all the evidence that has hitherto reached us upon the subject, *e.g.* the statements of Mr. Longcast (Note 32) or the following extract from a letter (*Natal Colonist*, Nov. 8) by ' a late visitor to Zululand,' dated Nov. 7, 1879 :—

the people who were supposed to abhor him as a cruel tyrant and to long only to be released from his bloody rule—it is painful to read the highly-coloured language in which Sir B. Frere in the Blue-Books labours at this point, again and again repeating his invectives and piling up his epithets, until at one time, no doubt, he succeeded in prejudicing the minds of the Government and People in England against the unfortunate King, whom from the very first and long before the raids occurred which have been put forward as the chief *casus belli*, he was, it is very plain, preparing to crush (Note 13).

Thus Sir B. Frere speaks of the 'grinding despotism' of 'their cruel Sovereign' [2222, p. 5], 'his faithless, cruel character' [*Ib*. p. 29], 'his atrocious barbarities' [2260, p. 24]—of the 'irresponsible, bloodthirsty, and treacherous despot' [2369, p. 1],

'On the highlands I found that, although the natives fully accept their defeat, they give excuses for every battle they have lost. *They speak in affectionate terms of their absent King*.' But the very same *Guardian*, which reports Mr. Cross's speech, contradicts it by the following from the Correspondent of the *Times*, dating from 'Utrecht'—'Had Cetshwayo been a tyrant hated of the people and reigning over them against their will, it would never have taken all the labour we experienced to capture him.'

the 'bloodthirsty, aggressive despot' [2316, p. 20],
'Cetshwayo's power of murder and plunder' [2269,
p. 1], 'the present despotism of a ruthless savage'
[2318, p. 51], the 'ignorant and bloodthirsty despot,' who is only 'anxious to emulate the sanguinary
fame of his uncle Chaka' [*Ib.* p. 214], whose 'history
is written in characters of blood' [p. 183], whose
'murders and massacres are simply part of a settled
purpose to imitate Chaka' [*Ib.*]—'in cruelty and
treachery he is no degenerate representative of Chaka
and Dingane,' 'with Chaka as his avowed model'
[*Ib.* p. 6]—'the monster Chaka is his model, to
emulate Chaka in shedding blood is, as far as I have
heard, his highest aspiration' [2220, p. 26]—'we
have not a shadow of excuse for doubting that he is
in his later utterances expressing his real intention
to resume the most sanguinary of his predecessors'
practices' [*Ib.*]—'he was, as I believe, inclined to
break loose from all restraint and to re-establish the
régime of Chaka's unmitigated barbarism' [2260,
p. 25], &c. &c. &c.

Nor am I aware of one single expression, in all
the numerous Despatches of Sir B. Frere printed in

the Blue-Books, which qualifies the above language, by recognizing some act or quality not altogether fiendish in one whom Englishmen generally, I trust, have learned by this time to know as a brave and not ignoble ruler—who had, of course, as Mr. Vijn says, ' to enforce from time to time the laws of his country, and, if he had not done so, where should I have been ? '—who never, since he began to reign, has sent his *Impi* on the war-path—who did his best to avoid war with the English, until it was forced upon him—who never used his opportunities for ravaging this Colony, when it lay at his mercy—who sent repeatedly messengers suing for peace, but only to be ' detained ' or ' manacled ' for weeks together by the English Authorities (Note 39), or sent back with the mockery of utterly impossible demands (Notes 37, 41), except the last (published in the *London Gazette* of Aug. 21), which never reached him (Note 46),—and who has been throughout hardly, ungenerously, and unjustly dealt with by the representatives of the English People.

It has been terrible to see this great wave of wickedness rolling on, and to be powerless to help it, to be debarred all possibility of showing the injustice of the war, until it was too late—too late to prevent the shedding of innocent blood and the ravaging of a whole country—too late to save the lives of 2,000 of our own soldiers and natives, and of 10,000 patriotic Zulus—too late to prevent the name of Englishman from becoming in the Native mind the synonym for duplicity, treachery, and violence, instead of, as in days gone by, for truth, and justice, and righteousness. The venerable South-African Missionary, Dr. Moffat, addressing a meeting on May 21, is reported (*Cape Argus*, June 17) to have condemned the Zulu War as ' brutal and unjust.' ' He had admired Sir B. Frere as a Christian ; but he never imagined that he would have precipitated the War as he did. With regard to the influence of the war on Missions, he believed that it would put them back at least 50 years in that part of the world.' With what face indeed can men teach Christianity to the Natives of these parts for many years to come, while they can point to such deeds of rapine and bloodshed, as done by the orders of Christian rulers, in the name of a Christian Nation, within the memory of living men ?

Dr. Moffat probably supposed at first, as some of us here did in Natal, that Sir B. Frere, after making a judicious exhibition on our frontier or, if need be, in Zululand itself, of the power of England, would have sought, by wise and peaceful measures of negotiation, to bring about gradually the desired improvements in the Military and Marriage Systems of Zululand, in accordance with the principle laid down by himself on another occasion [2079, p. 7] that 'such changes, like all great revolutions, require time and patience to effect peacefully ;' and there is every reason for believing that this work, worthy of the English Name, might have been done successfully. But we did not expect that, in order to accomplish these ends, he would direct a ferocious onslaught to be made on unprepared and unoffending Zulus, who were sitting quietly at their homes, ' cattle grazing on the hills, men, women, and children at their kraals, cows being milked' (Note 18) as usual, when, immediately after crossing the frontier, Lord Chelmsford's force swooped down upon them, and he reports his work for the first two days as 30 killed, 4 wounded, 10 captured, together with 13 horses, 413 cattle, 332 goats, 235 sheep ; while Col. Wood's captured 2,000 cattle.

I sympathise, in short, entirely with the words of a friend, who with full knowledge of the facts states his conviction that ' the Zulu War, discreditable to our arms, disgraceful to our civilization, and injurious to our good name and to the discipline of our army, was not necessary, and therefore was without just cause '—who is ' disgusted to hear (so calling themselves) Christians speak of cruel murders as if they were the finest feats of arms,' and who mournfully adds, ' It makes one despair of ultimate good, to see such a Saturnalia of wrongdoing and such an apotheosis of Force in this lower world.'

Cetshwayo is now a prisoner at Capetown,[1] sup-

[1] The following appears in the *Daily Telegraph* from its Spec. Corresp., dating ' Capetown, Sept. 23 ' (*Pall-Mall Gazette*, Oct. 10, 1879) :—

' Cetshwayo, now confined in the Castle, fully acknowledges that he has been properly punished. His statements most completely vindicate the policy of Sir B. Frere. He says that

plied, no doubt, with food and clothing and other comforts, but deprived of all such resources as

Shepstone was to blame for the war by annexing the Transvaal, and that, as England was bound to maintain the Transvaal dispute, he was equally bound not to disband his army. He would long have ceased to have been a King had he done so. He saw from the Whiteman's [point of] view how requisite it was that the military power of Zululand should be broken. He denies emphatically that at any time overtures were made to him to use his army against the Boers. This was the allegation which aroused such intense indignation through South Africa. The frankness of the King is extraordinary, and he seems quite content to pass the remainder of his life away from the cares of State.'

In reading the above it should remembered that all such communications must be regarded as having something of an *official* character ; since no English *friend* of Cetshwayo is allowed to speak with him on political matters, or in most cases (from want of acquaintance with the Zulu tongue) would be able to converse with him at all, except through the Government interpreter. Mr. F. E. Colenso, who speaks Zulu freely, on his way to England requested permission to see Cetshwayo, who had just arrived at the Cape, but was refused by Sir Bartle Frere, on the ground that Sir G. Wolseley's leave must first be obtained, 'to whom all applications to communicate with the prisoner should be referred ' ; though at the very same time the Editor of the *Cape Times* (Government organ) had a long—it is said a two-hours'—interview with him. In fact, the above statement bears a curious resemblance to a series of telegrams from Capetown and other communications from these parts, which appeared in English Journals during some months before hostilities began against the Zulus, and were evidently intended to create a prejudice against Cetshwayo, as if he had been threatening and aggressive towards Natal, and so to prepare the English People for the war. I drew attention at the time to some of these false and misleading telegrams, &c. in a letter to the *Daily News.*

relieve the weary hours of civilized men—utterly cut off from friends and country, except a few followers (two men and four girls, but none of his wives) imprisoned with him—surrounded by Whitemen, but unable to exchange a single idea with them, except through a half-caste interpreter; while the name of the only Whiteman who, he believes, would be willing and able to speak a word for him, is not allowed to be mentioned before him, as it ' excites the prisoner.' Through an order from Sir G. Wolseley, however, I sent a message to say ' Sobantu salutes Cetshwayo—he is grieved for him—he does not forget him '; and I received this message in reply, ' Cetshwayo thanks Sobantu for his message, and is glad to learn that he does not forget him. He hopes Sobantu will speak well for him.' In this little book I have spoken the truth on his behalf, and collected some important and striking evidence, which shows, as indeed does each fresh piece of evidence which comes to light, that he has not deserved the treatment he has received. But there he lies—in spirit bound hand and foot, and gagged—awaiting his judgment at the hands of the

English People. May God grant that for their own sakes, as well as for that of the Zulus—for the raising up again of England's good name among the tribes of South Africa, who stand aghast at our recent doings—they may do what is just and right towards them in the name of Him of whom it is written—-

> 'A GOD OF TRUTH AND WITHOUT INIQUITY,
> JUST AND RIGHT IS HE!'

J. W. NATAL.

BISHOPSTOWE: *Nov.* 16, 1879.

a

PRIVATE JOURNAL

CETSHWAYO'S DUTCHMAN.

———◦◦———

Oct. 29, 1878.—I set out from New Guelderland [1] with six Natal Kafirs, one wagon, sixteen oxen,
and a load of goods, consisting of woollen blankets,
baize blankets, lined [2] cotton blankets, picks, knives,
beads, saddles and bridles, &c., for Zululand, in order
to trade for cattle and hides. Having started about
10 A.M., and the weather being rainy, I could not
get further than the Isinkwazi River, after crossing
the Nonoti River.

At the store and canteen, belonging to Mr. W.
Weber, and built on the N.W. side of the river
nearly up to the crown of a hill, I outspanned my
oxen to let them graze, the ground being for the

[1] *New Guelderland*, a Dutch settlement in Natal, near the
coast, about thirteen miles from the Zulu Border.

[2] *Lined Cotton Blankets—i.e.* calico sheets, lined or covered
with coloured handkerchiefs

most part free for anyone—at all events, for travellers. I told my Kafirs to prepare their food, which
consisted of ground mealies (maize) and salt; and I
said further that at sundown the oxen must be tied
to their yokes to prevent their running away. I
myself went to Mr. W. W.'s house, to remain there
until the next morning. There I met a certain Mr.
B., who wished me to take his oxen among my herd
to his son in Zululand. I was quite willing to do so,
but was obliged to require that they should be with
me early next morning, as I wanted to go on, and
should not wish to be kept waiting. Mr. B. promised
this, and thereupon set off, as did also Mr. W. W.,
for New Guelderland, so that I and Tony Weber remained behind together. After sundown, not knowing what else to do, and there being moonlight, we
saddled two horses and took a little turn. We came
back about 9 P.M., and, after supper, lay down to sleep.

Oct. 30.—Next morning I was up and about
an hour before sunrise. Of course my first care was
my oxen, to loose them and let them get their morning feed; for I meant to inspan about an hour after
sunrise, and outspan across the Tugela (or Border)
River, not supposing that I should be disappointed
through Mr. B. of carrying out my intention of
making an early start. At 9 A.M. no oxen were to

be seen, at noon it was just the same, at sundown
still there were no oxen of Mr. B. As I did not wish
to go back from my promise to take the oxen under
my charge to his son, I determined still to wait the
following day till 2 P.M., and, if they had not arrived
by that time, I would then go on without them.

Oct. 31.—This morning the weather was quite
different from yesterday's, the sun giving signs of an
exceedingly hot day, whereas yesterday it was not
visible.

There was very little news here. Only a gossip
went round about a war between the Zulus and the
English being near at hand. But, as I had only
lately returned from Zululand, and had left everything quiet there, except that now and then a great
hunting party was held among themselves, and as
the war-talk was mere rumour and had been current
for the last two years(1),[1] I gave little heed to it.

Before I was at all aware it was $2\frac{1}{2}$ P.M. And,
as still none of Mr. B.'s oxen had appeared, I told
my Kafirs to inspan, as I meant to sleep on this side
of the Tugela. But, before I had gone two miles, I
was met by two native policemen, carrying a large
official letter addressed to myself. To open and
read it was, of course, only a matter of a few minutes·

[1] The figures in parentheses refer to notes at end of book.

It contained little of special importance for me, no-thing more, in fact, than that it came from the Border Agent (Mr. Jackson), who, having heard that I was on my way to Zululand, had sent these two policemen to meet me with this letter, notifying that my wagon could not pass until the Border Agent had first examined it, *i.e.* for smuggled goods, as guns, &c. After examining my goods, he signed my pass and I was allowed to go on. But Mr. Jackson told me that danger was threatening from the Zulu side of the Tugela, not from the Natal side, referring, no doubt, to the ' hunting parties,' which the King had ordered, to show that he had an army as well as the Whites, but not with any intention of invading Natal.

Just about sundown I reached the Tugela, which this year contained very little water, and was now so low that I had no need to be taken over by boats. However I remained that night on this (Natal) side of the river.

I went myself to the house of an acquaintance (a Hollander) to spend the evening with him. Our conversation was about the war so likely to come about. My friend thought it rather venturesome in me to make my way through to the Zulus; ' for,' said he, ' should the war break out while you are

there, assuredly you will then be a dead man, your
end will be frightful, to be put to death by the
greatest and fiercest of Zulu savages.' I, however,
lightminded and determined as ever, crossed over
next morning at daybreak. Having once resolved on
anything, no earthly power should dissuade me from
it.

Nov. 1.—Early this morning, about 9 A.M., I was
across the Tugela with wagon and oxen, having got
through the river and reached the top of the hill,
without the wagon once sticking fast. After out-
spanning for half an hour, we inspanned and went
on, meaning to outspan again about six miles further
on. The road here went through an open bush-
country, but very far from flat; on the contrary we
had to go up and down several high hills. When we
had left about three miles behind us, I came across
a number of Zulu women, their only clothing being,
as usual, a piece of dressed ox-hide or cloth fastened
about the middle, the married women or marriageable girls being distinguished by a red top-knot on
the back of their heads, and carrying their children
on their backs. My attention, however, would not
have been drawn to them but for the strange
performance in which they were engaged. These
women, in fact, were all collected together in one

spot, singing, shouting, laughing, crying, clapping
their hands, now standing still, then again briskly
running, and so on. As this was all new for me, I
asked my own natives what it all meant. They told
me that this was a method of *asking for rain*. And
truly here, in these parts, the last years have been
unusually dry. The season was already half over;
no rain would come; all the young crops, which had
sprouted out of the ground, were burnt through the
heat of the sun and drought. The men and young
men of Zululand had all been called up to the King
for some reason or other (2), what we knew not—
although in Natal it was thought they were coming
over to attack the Whites. And so the women had
been left by themselves alone in the land, to look
after the huts and take care of the cattle and gardens. When, however, the males are at home, they
do little or nothing; their women are as good as
slaves for them; they have to prepare food for the
males and to cook beer for them; almost everything
is left for the women to do. The work of the men
consists solely in slaughtering cattle, milking, hunting, war;[1] they pass the time also in chatting with

[1] Since Cetshwayo came to the throne (Sept. 1, 1873) the
Zulus have never once been engaged in war, until the British
forces invaded Zululand (Jan. 11, 1879). His father Mpande
(Panda), however, ravaged repeatedly the Swazis and other
native tribes.

the girls; as they do not eat fish, they make no attempt to catch them.

By this time I had outspanned again, the oxen being soon tired, as the sun was very hot. When they were outspanned, there came a middle-aged man and a young man of about 20 years, to lounge by me at the wagon. These two were very much surprised to see a Whiteman enter Zululand with a wagon laden with goods. Accordingly they asked me ' whither I was going ? and how was it possible that I could have entered the land with an honest purpose of trading, when the war was so near at hand, and might break out any day ? ' I replied that ' I had nothing to do with the war and knew nothing whatever about it. But I was going to sell to the King for cattle the goods in the wagon, since the King had sent for me.' With this they were satisfied, but it was far otherwise with me. I asked them ' Inasmuch as they had told me that the war might break out at any day, had they heard anything? and had the King, then, called up his people to go and fight in Natal ? ' They said that this was not the case. Cetshwayo had called up his people in order to consult with them what course they should take; since the greedy and stubborn Boers were on their way to fight with them in their own land (3), and take away their cattle and girls. But they positively had no intention of fighting against their own (English) people.'

After this conversation I took my mid-day meal, consisting of rice and milk, with a piece of dry bread and a cup of coffee with sugar. Then the oxen were inspanned, as I meant to pass the night at a place about eight miles further on, where there was good feeding-ground by the Umsundusi River.

Among the young warriors, however, at this time there was much braggadocio talk about crossing over into Natal and building a kraal at Stanger, where Chaka's grave was (4), a Military Kraal opposite to the English Kraal where the Resident Magistrate lived. But the King had no wish to invade Natal, and would not allow them to do so; and, though he agreed that the land north of the Umvoti River belonged properly to Zululand, yet he said 'he did not want it, and had no desire to fight with the English.'

Nov. 2.—Splendid weather in the morning, though in the afternoon the sky was overcast. Trekked across the Inyezane River, and there passed the night.

Nov. 3.—Went on to Etshowe,[1] an excellent place

[1] This name (of the Rev. Mr. Oftebro's station) is often misspelt '*Ekowe*,' the error having arisen from the fact that the Norwegian missionaries use a letter somewhat like *k* to represent the sound *tsh.*

for cattle. Here I rested about six days, because the grass was particularly good, and my cattle had need of it, being very thin.

From the time when I crossed over from Natal I had only traded two head of cattle. At this place I was summoned by Dabulamanzi to come to his kraal with my wagon and goods, since he wished to buy goods of me for gold and cattle. But, as I knew him very well as an uncommonly sharp customer, I was not disposed to go to his place, which was about three hours distant from here. So I told his man that, 'if his master wished to buy anything from me, he must come to me, since his place was out of the way and my oxen were very thin.'

Nov. 4.—Next day Dabulamanzi himself made his appearance with his following. On arriving he first asked for spirits, and I gave him a good glass of rum. Then he began to talk with me about goods, and said that ' he wished very much to see the stuff which I had in the wagon.' Of course I let him see all, and I then presented him with a good shawl, whereupon he made me a present of 20*s.* Before he went away, however, he would make me promise to bring my wagon to his kraal next morning. He then took another glass of rum, and with his following set out on his return.

Nov. 5.—The next day the oxen were inspanned
in order to keep my promise according to agree-
ment. About noon we came to his kraal 'Ezulwini,'
not far from Bishop Schreuder's Mission Station.
As soon as I arrived he sent me a fine young beast
for an old debt, and two hours afterwards he came
himself to the wagon with two of his men. He
first said that he wished to buy from me the piece
of black [baize (52 yards), and I had to unroll it for
him, and say how many blankets he could cut out
of it. He then wished to give me 4s. a yard for it,
since, as he said, it cost no more than that in
Durban. Of course I could not do this, nor could
I make him understand that I must have something
for bringing it into Zululand. This not having
been made clear to him, he wished to buy picks,
but wanted forty for a cow. Of course I could not
agree to this, and so in the end he bought nothing.
However, he still had a great deal to say about all
sorts of things, about trade, and about the approaching war. According to his ideas, since they
had now as good weapons as the Whites, they would
be stronger than the English; for the King was
abundantly supplied with powder and lead and caps,
and, even should the powder come to an end, this
would be no such great hindrance, since there were

Zulus enough who could themselves make powder; so that they would have no want of ammunition for six years to come.

Nov. 6.—Next morning I put the oxen again to the wagon. Just as we were inspanning came Mr. Dabulamanzi once more to the wagon, in order, as he said, to bid me farewell; he said further 'if I could not sell my goods, I must come back to him, and he would then buy everything from me'—of course at his own price. Dabulamanzi, though a sharp trader and fond of a glass of gin or rum, is held in much respect by the Zulus.

From this place I went back just past one of the King's Kraals which is built there. Here I bought two sacks of mealies for my Kafirs, and a fine young beast from the Inkosikazi (head-woman). It was a rainy day and few Zulus were to be seen. But before evening there came a Zulu well known to me, and asked, as many had done, about the war. I replied, as always, that 'I knew of no war, but had come in to trade.' He asked me 'Where would I trade, since all the Zulus had gone up to the King, and the White Troops were already at the Tugela, with the purpose of presently entering Zululand?' I replied that 'I knew, of course, that the Zulus had gone up to the King; but I had no knowledge that the soldiers had come to the Border.' But I did not suppose that there was much danger in this, as I thought that they had only come to the Border to protect the Whites in case the Zulus should think of coming over into Natal. I had no fear, therefore, of war and went forward.

After giving my oxen another two days' rest I went on to Nodada's, a place on this bank of the Umhlatuze River. From here I sent back two of my people to Natal, to get a little information about the war. After they had started we had a terrific thundershower, so heavy as I had very rarely seen. I set off from here and went across the river, where I intended to wait for my Kafirs, who would not return very quickly. Another of my Kafirs was so ill that I was obliged to send him back to his family, where, as I heard afterwards, he died.

At the end of four days my Kafirs came back from Natal with a letter from home in which my friend wrote that 'the soldiers, it is true, had come to the Border, but it would probably be some time yet before the war would break out, and I had better go on and buy cattle, since they were at a high price and would become still dearer.' So I went on fearlessly; since Mr. Dunn was also still in Zululand, I saw no danger in advancing further.

On the following days there was little news, nothing but rain and wind, so that travelling was now far from pleasant. There was here an extraordinary demand for mealies among the Zulus, who wished to buy for cattle, since they had very few in store, and their gardens also promised no early and profitable harvest.

Nov. 17.—I met Mr. John Dunn not far from Kwamagwaza. Going from my wagon to his, I asked information from him about the war, and whether it was dangerous to go on. He replied that 'the Whites would not cross the Border, and Cetshwayo would soon come to good terms with the English. But,' Mr. Dunn said, 'you must not listen to the soldiers of the young regiments, who are rather insolent, but do no real harm.' I was thus set at rest about the war by a person who in my opinion must know all about the state of things within Zululand and without, and who, no doubt, did know thoroughly.

Nov. 19.—Two days afterwards the Zulus would not let me pass on, because I would not buy their hides. But, when I told them that the goods in the wagon belonged to the King, they had their mouths soon shut, and I went on without any kind of hindrance.

Nov. 24.—Crossed the White Imvolosi, and just in time; if I had been one hour later, I should have been altogether too late. For, when I had got through the river and had outspanned, the clouds gathered together, and a heavy thunderstorm, accompanied with a downpour of rain, burst over the earth, and at the end of two hours the river was so full that it was dangerous for man or beast to swim across.

At this time the Zulus were all dispersing again to their kraals.[1] In a few days a party of chief men were to set out for the Lower Tugela in order to talk about the war. Of course, all that I now got to hear came from the people, and so I can answer very little for the truth of it all. Unfortunately I knew no longer what day of the month it was; for I had lost my reckoning, and, having no almanac I could no more set myself right.[2]

[1] 'The greater part of the men ordered to the King's Kraal some time back have returned to their homes, in many instances without being regularly dismissed. They express great dissatisfaction at the conduct of the King, *having been set to hoe his crops, instead of being sent out to war,* as they expected—and this without food, as he allows them nothing: all they eat must be brought from their homes.'—Mr. Robson, Border Agent, Dec. 5, 1878 [2308, p. 22].

[2] Sir H. Bulwer's message of Nov. 16—announcing his intention of sending one or more Government officers to the Drift of the Lower Tugela, there to 'deliver the words of the decision' in respect to the disputed territory, 'together with such other words on other questions as H.E. the High Commissioner may de-

The Zulus were very friendly towards me, and trade was unusually good. Chief men came to me continually, both to buy and to talk over the now-impending war. The main part of the talk of the persons of most importance and of the people was that the Whites[1] 'were very bad people. Since they had only just before set the King upon the throne, why had they now come to fight with him, in order to kill him and take away his country from him ? ' In fact, the Zulus had the idea that the Whites had come to capture all the males, to be sent to England and there kept to work, while the girls would be all married off to (white) soldiers, and their cattle would, of course, all belong to the English Government. Hence, when it came to fighting, they fought not for the King only, but for themselves, since they would rather die than live under the Whites.

According to my notion it was now December 20. I had left the Emahlabatini[2] district, not out

sire to have conveyed at the same time—may have reached the King about Nov. 24, so that Mr. Vijn, who had 'lost his reckoning,' may be here referring to what he had heard from the people about Nov. 28–30.

[1] By the 'Whites' (*abelungu*) the Zulus meant the ' English, the Boers being distinguished as *ama Bunu.*

[2] The locality in which the Royal Kraal Ulundi is, or rather was, situated.

of any fear of the natives or want of good trade, but through want of food. No mealies or Kafir-corn, no milk or beer, could I buy here, so that I was obliged to go on further in the hope of finding food.

Two days afterwards (December 22) I reached the Great Kraals on the other side of the Black Imvolosi, whither I had sent in advance one of my Kafirs; and so, as soon as I had outspanned, I speedily bought mealies, and on the very next day I had bought so much that I was in a position to purchase a beast for mealies.

The weather was daily excessively bad, rain and wind, the rivers always overflowing their banks.

There was very little news about the war. According to report, the persons who had been sent by Cetshwayo to the Lower Tugela had not yet come back(5). Also I now became aware that the Whites had demanded from Cetshwayo three or four persons—Assegai (Sihayo)(6), Mehlokazulu, Nkumbikazulu, and Umbilini. A council had been held about the surrender of these persons. The Chief men generally, and most of the King's brothers, *e.g.* Hamu, Ziwedu, Siteku, and some others, were of opinion, and desired, that the persons demanded by the English should be seized and surrendered. But Cetshwayo and the Zulus were of quite another opinion; so also were Dabulamanzi, Zibebu, and Maduna the King's full brother. They thought that these persons should on no account be given up; ' since the Whites would here be only acting in their usual fashion, and, very probably, when these had been given up, they would again demand others, and therefore it was better to fight at once, since it evidently must come to that.'

What the King may have said on the return of the Chief men sent by him, I know not, since I was not with him. But I do know that, when the Chief men (Sintwangu, Vumandaba, &c.) had returned, 600 or 800 cattle must have been collected, which, according to what I heard, were being sent by the King to Natal, to pay for the persons demanded by the Government(7); but these cattle, as I was told, were driven back by the Zulus, and slaughtered and stolen, not far from Kwamagwaza. The Zulus, when they were with the King, refused to agree with the chief men, and said that they would take the four persons into their midst, and die together fighting against the English. In this state of things what had the poor King to do? The report came that the English were over the Border. Of course he sent out his host to fight; one part, the

largest, was sent to the Buffalo River, the other
portion to the coast.

At the end of the year 1878 I sent one of my
Kafirs to James Rorke, who kept a store at Hamu's.
Two or three days afterwards, about sundown, he
came with his man to my wagon, both on horseback.
We had much to talk about that night; for certainly our position was anything but pleasant; if
war began between the Zulus and the Whites, very
probably we also should be made shorter by a head.
In the morning we went back together to his (J.
Rorke's) place, partly to have some more conversation
with each other, partly because a good horse was for
sale in the neighbourhood, which I was minded to
buy, so that, in case of need, I might make my way
out as quickly as possible. When we came to the
place (Reintorf's old Mission Station[1]) I found there
the person who had the horse for sale; he spoke
with me about the price, and promised to send for
the horse that same day, since it was not at his

[1] 'I further desire to inform Y. E. (Sir G. Wolseley) that
another station, " Esihlengeni," situate near Hamu's head-kraal,
during the absence of the Rev. Reinsdorf on duty, was also
taken possession of by one James Rorke, under the plea that
permission had been granted to him by Hamu, and he refused to
give the same up on Mr. Reinsdorf's demand.'—Rev. K. Holhs,
Superintendent of Hermansburg Hanoverian Missions, Sept 8,
1879.

house. I looked out for it day after day, but
nothing appeared. At last, after six days, the message came back that the person who had the horse
in keeping for the owner wished first to have his
expenses paid before giving back the horse. The
owner, therefore, sent back again the same day, because I was in haste, and wished to have the animal
speedily, as I purposed to return back to Natal.

A secret message came from Hamu (Oham)(8)
that James Rorke must get all ready for a flight.
His Kafirs must carry all their goods to hiding-
places, and the cattle must be collected, the news
being that the Whites had come over into Zululand.[1]

According to my reckoning it was about January
10, 1879, when two of my Kafirs, who had been left
at the wagon, set out from it and came to me in the
morning with tidings that ' I must be at the wagon
that very day, since Zulus had come from the
King's place, who had one or more messages for me.'
What was I to do ? A horse was speedily borrowed
with a Kafir, who should bring it back the next
morning. On that day before sundown I reached

---

[1] Colonel Wood crossed into Zululand, and so began the
Invasion, on Jan. 6, 1879 [2242, p. 19], whereas the thirty days
allowed in the Ultimatum ended on Jan. 10.

my wagon, where I found seven Zulus, who said
that 'they had been sent by the King with a notice
that I was to collect my cattle and goods, wagon
and oxen, whatever I had, and they were to take me
to the King's kraal, and then the King would give
me other men to accompany me to Natal, so that,
as I had only come to trade, no harm might befall
me in his land.'

All this seemed certainly very nice and good.
But why, then, had they taken away my weapons?
If they had nothing in view with regard to us, they
ought not to have done this. Should I try to get
these back with pleasant talk or with threats? All
in vain! they would not give them back to me,
because 'they were afraid that I should shoot them!'
No! they would not give back to me a single gun,
and said that 'I must now go and sleep, and they
would come back to me next morning and say what
I must do.' Seeing that I could do nothing else, I
went and lay down to sleep under the wagon after a
cup of coffee.

Next morning, half-an-hour after sunrise, the
Zulus came to the wagon and said that 'I must have
the oxen inspanned within half-an-hour, and also
must have all my cattle collected within an hour.'
While we were packing the goods in the wagon and

inspanning the oxen, I heard the Impi (armed party) whispering among themselves, and made out that they had not been sent by the King at all, but by Zibebu, son of the late Mapita. When the wagon was inspanned, the Impi went to the kraal where they had slept, to get their blankets and mats. As soon as they had gone I went forward with the wagon on the way to the King. I had not gone more than two miles when the Impi came running fast and crying after me saying that 'I must stop! Where was I going? This was not the way by which they would and must take me. And where were all my cattle?' I replied that 'I was on my way to the King, and my cattle had been all along at Ulundi, because here I had no pasture.' They replied that 'the King and his people had marched out to go and fight with the English, since the Whites had crossed the Border, and taken away all the cattle at the point of the assegai(9); and they (the Impi) had been ordered to take me and all my belongings into Zibebu's country, and every one of my Kafirs must go away to Natal.' I saw now only too plainly that they had no good intentions towards me, but would kill me in some uninhabited place.

Two Zulus, who worked for me, were now driven away with assegais and sticks. Four of my Natal

Kafirs I had sent away secretly to the King,' to tell him what they were doing with me and my goods, for I could not believe that the King had any evil purpose towards me. After they were gone the Impi became more mischievous and insolent than ever, saying that 'I must turn round with my wagon, and must deliver to them my cattle, since they knew very well that I had plenty of cattle here.' But I sturdily refused and would not give ear to their demand. I had now only two Kafirs left, and ordered these to outspan the oxen from the wagon; but they seemed afraid to do so. I got down, therefore, from the wagon and began to outspan the oxen. But, as soon as I began, the Impi came to me and asked ' Did I wish to be killed?' I said ' If they meant to take my life, they had only got to do it, and the sooner the better.' Then they asked ' Was I a stone, then, that they could not kill me? or, when dead, would I come to life again?' I said that ' I was not afraid of death, and they might do what they would.' Then I whispered to my two Kafirs that they had best take to flight and leave me behind alone. But they seemed to have no mind for that, and asked me ' Why did I not listen to the Impi, since Zibebu certainly would not kill us?' But I said that ' Zibebu was only too well

known to me,[1] and I had no mind to go to his
country.' Then I went and lay down upon the grass,
to see what would be done with us. My two Kafirs,
urged by fear, went away with the Impi and the
wagon and oxen; they went also and took my cattle
out of the different kraals where I had placed them,
and gave them to the Impi, leaving me behind in
the grass without blanket and without food. In
two hours' time all had disappeared out of my sight,
and I was quite alone, among savages, who at any
instant might put me to death! However, some
good-natured Zulus pitied me, and took me into
one of their kraals, lent me a new blanket, gave me
a mat and enough to eat, consisting of beer and
amasi (sour-milk), and mealies ground between two
stones.

What now should I do? What part of the world
should I strike for, the Bombo Mountains[2] or Natal?
The first course was nearest and least dangerous;
the last was impossible, since thus very probably I
should meet Cetshwayo's war-parties, and then certainly it would be all over with me.

[1] Zibebu as well as Hamu, is one of the thirteen chiefs appointed by Sir G. Wolseley to be rulers in Zululand.

[2] The Bombo Mountains are the eastern boundary of Swaziland, separating between the Swazis and Tongas, and running
down south into Zululand.

The next day I sent one of my Zulus back to Hamu (for my two Zulus had come back to me again in the afternoon of the previous day) to borrow a horse from him. Two days later my young man came back with the message that 'he (Hamu) was very sorry that one of his horses had died two days previously; but he would be very glad if I would come to him on foot, and he might afterwards, perhaps, manage to procure a horse for me.' On the same day when this message arrived, someone brought a report that the Zulu King had put to death four Natal natives, that is, as I supposed, my own four men. But afterwards I found that they were quite safe and sound, and I believe that the whole story was false, and that the King had not killed any Natal Kafirs.

What was I to do now—alone in a savage land, among rough, unfeeling, uncivilised natives? Only three faithful Zulus remained with me, who agreed to take me to Hamu's country, where my friend James Rorke was still staying.

Next day we began our journey, the distance being not less than forty miles, through high hills and thickets. When we had gone about ten miles there came a native crying after us and bidding us to stop. I asked resolutely for an assegai from one

of my attendants, intending, if need be, to sell
my life as dearly as possible. Being all ready,
when the Kafir came near, I recognised him as
one of my own men, whom I had sent to the Zulu
King.

As soon as he came to me I went and sat on the
grass with him, to hear what news he had to tell.
He had come to the King, with my other three servants, just at the time when Cetshwayo had sent out
his army in two divisions to meet the Whites, one
to Isandhlwana, and the other to the coast. When
the King heard how his people had treated me he was
astounded, and said that this had occurred without
his order or cognizance. Then he agreed with his
chief men and brothers that no harm must be done
to me, and that all my goods must be collected and
brought back to me. Thereupon he sent with my
Kafirs two of his own Indunas, with the order that
my wagon, oxen, goods and cattle, all of them, should
be brought together—that I too, the Whiteman,
should be taken to one of his own kraals, with all
my belongings—that no one must dare to touch me
or my property, since I, and all I had, belonged from
that moment to the King until the war should be
over, when I might return in quiet to Natal again.
This Kafir, who had come in advance, had been sent

forward to see how I had fared, and to protect me from any further rough attack.

Glad was I when this had thus far come about happily for me, though I knew not what might befall me later on. But, trusting in my good star, I returned to the place where so much trouble had come upon me. On arrival I found that I had still a young beast left to me in one of the neighbouring kraals, which I sent for and gave as food for my people and the two King's Indunas, since they were hungry and I had nothing else for them to eat, for the Zulus had carried off my food as well as everything else that I possessed. The beast was slaughtered about 4 P.M., just when my other men had arrived with the King's Indunas to bring everything back to me. At all events they could now see something to eat, for they were very hungry.

Next morning I set out with two of my young Zulus for the place which the King had appointed for me; while the rest of my people went in the direction in which the Zulus with my goods had gone. I reached the place appointed towards evening, viz. a small kraal close to, and under the shadow of, the Royal Kraal Umbelebele, it was well known to me, as also the natives of that place knew me well. On my arrival they raised a great lamentation over me; but they wondered that the Zulus had not killed me. Then they enquired how all had happened, and by whose order; whereupon I told them all that I thought proper to tell them, to which they listened with attention, amazement, and disgust. When I had ended my story, they brought me a pot of Kafir beer, which I very soon put inside me.

Two days after I came here my wagon and oxen, goods and blankets, were brought back. Also my people, with the help of the two King's Indunas, had got back into their hands my plundered cattle. But, when they came near, I very soon said that my two Natal Kafirs, who had gone away with the wagons &c. were not there. On arriving, the first words, with which the other Kafirs greeted me, were that ' Mubi and Sopiti had been killed by the Zulus in the bush of the Black Imvolosi River, one of them shot, the other assegaid.' I asked ' Why had they left the wagon ? ' My Kafirs replied that ' the Zulus had told them that they had gone with the Impi because the Impi had promised to take them to Zibebu, who would assuredly see that they returned safe and sound to Natal. But, when they reached the Black Imvolosi, they were at once put to death, without any notice to the world.' And this, doubtless, would have been my fate also, if I had gone with them.

All my property had now been brought back, except my three fire-arms, two blankets, and some small goods, with three sacks of corn. They had found the oxen and cattle scattered over the whole district, three or four together; the wagon they had found at a kraal, whose inhabitants had used it as a house, thinking that they were now become as good as whites.

Jan. 21.—No news on this or the three following days.

Jan. 25.—About 2 P.M., while I lay in the hut, talking with one of the men of Ziwedu (Cetshwayo's brother), who had been sent by the King to learn about me, whether I was alive, and how it went with me, our attention was drawn to a troop of people, who came back from their gardens crying and wailing. As they approached, I recognised them as persons belonging to the kraal in which I was staying. When they came into or close to the kraal, they kept on wailing in front of the kraals, rolling themselves on the ground and never quieting down; nay, in the night they wailed so as to cut through the heart of anyone. And this wailing went on, night and day, for a fortnight; the effect of it was very depressing; I wished I could not hear it.

The reason of this was that the headman of the

Kraal, Msundusi, a trusty person and the husband
of four wives, had fallen in the fight at ISANDHL-
WANA. It is true, on that day, the Zulus over-
powered the Whites, and killed them in a way which
my pen cannot describe, more than 1,200 Whites
having been there put to death in a dreadful manner. But also of the Zulus, according to their
account, many thousands had been left behind on
the field—Dabulamanzi told me they were buried—
never more to return to their homes, and still more
were wounded.[1]

On this same day also (January 22) the English
on the Coast fought a battle with the Zulus,[2] when
the Whites routed the Zulus to and over the Umhlatuze River, where the Zulus held their ground in
the bush. The Whites now began to build a fort
at Etshowe, an old Mission Station (Mr. Oftebro's).

Rough and dangerous were the times which now
broke for me. Repeatedly there came a hundred
Zulus, with uplifted spear-points flying at me, and

[1] Mehlokazulu, when examined at Maritzburg (Note 6),
stated, 'I heard that about 300 Zulus were killed at Rorke's
Drift. It is not known how many hundreds were killed at
Isandhlwana; there might have been 1,000 killed there. They
were buried in the mealie-pits in two kraals, some in *dongas*
(gullies) and elsewhere. Zulus died all round Isandhlwana.'

[2] This was the battle fought by Colonel Pearson's force at
the Innyezane River.

threatening to kill me, 'the white dog,' and then to
cut me in pieces. Sometimes, in fact, they were
almost crying with rage, wanting to kill me. But
each time they were afraid of the King's Indunas.

The King was very glad when he heard that his
people had gained the victory over the Whites, and
thought that the war would now be at an end, supposing that the Whites had no more soldiers.[1] His
people, or rather a portion only of his people, brought
to him the oxen and cattle captured from the Whites,
as also some wagons—I saw only an ambulance-
wagon—and two cannons, about which they were
wild with delight. But the greater part of the
booty, as blankets, fire-arms, cartridges, clothes,
gold, had been carried home to their own places by
most of the Zulus,[2] at which the King was much

[1] 'The Zulus told me that, after the Battle of Isandhlwana,
John Dunn sent a message to the King that 'he must send
his army to the coast, and, if he beat the Whitemen there, he
would be all right, for the Whitemen would then be finished off,
since the Army on the coast was all they had left.'—C. Vijn.

[2] 'Only two cannon were taken to Cetshwayo. They remained on the field a long time—I should think about 10
days—and then they were sent for by the King, and brought
down in a wagon.

'Only four wagons were taken to the King; but Matshana
took a number of wagons, and Sihayo four.

'Each man helped himself to matches and such other property as they could lay hands upon and carry away.

'Each man also helped himself to ammunition. The cases

displeased. The King was angered also because his
people had gone over the Zulu Border into Natal;
for he said ' It is the Whites who have come to fight
with me in my own country, and not I that go to
fight with them. My intention, therefore, is only
to defend myself in my own country, where they
themselves made me King a few years ago (10).'

The King's army on the coast was stationed at
the Umhlatuze River, from which they came, from
time to time, to fight with the Whites at Etshowe,
where they kept them for two months entirely shut
up, purposing to starve them out.

According to report there came about this time
a Tonga doctor to the Zulu King, offering his ser-
vices, viz. for killing the Whites by poisoning the
springs of water for them. But the King would not
listen to this. He said that 'he would not fight
with the Whites in any such inhuman manner, but
he would fight in honourable fashion, for he had
men enough for this (11). Also he gave orders
always to his people that, 'whenever they were able
to get Whitemen into their hands alive, they were
not to kill them, but must bring them to him.'

At a certain time—I think, in the end of February
of guns and ammunition were smashed open and broken with
stones. It (the ammunition) is in the country; we have returned some of it.'—*Mehlokazulu.*

or beginning of March, but I cannot remember the time exactly—the rumour went through the country that Hamu had gone over to the Whites with his people and cattle.   Hamu, in fact, had from the first been opposed to going to war with the Whites, and had advised that it was best to give up the men demanded by the English Government, to which, as I have already said, the Zulus would not agree. Hence Hamu now went over.

Different accounts reached me about this running away of Hamu.   At one time, it would seem, he had shut himself up in an underground mountain-cave, so that other chief men came to beguile him with talk, asking 'why he went over to the Whites, and what harm they (the Zulus) had done to him, since he had always been a great and prominent person in Zululand'(12), adding that 'if he of his own accord came out of the cave, no harm would be done to him.'   At another time it was said that Hamu had been caught and brought back to Cetshwayo.   But nothing seemed to be certain.   At all events Hamu got safe and sound to the Whites. Then they told me that on his arrival the Whites had stripped off his head-ring, and all his women and girls had been married off to Natal natives.[1]

[1] There was no truth whatever in this report, nor in the

On its being reported that Hamu had deserted
to the Whites, the order went round from the King
immediately that his people (soldiers) must come
up to pursue after Hamu, and bring him back alive
or dead. In this pursuit various atrocities were
committed. All, old or young, who refused food to
them, were killed by the Zulu force, now an old
man, now an old woman, now a young girl. When
the Zulus saw that Hamu was not to be caught,
they went back to the King. He was much vexed
that Hamu had not been brought a captive, but
said 'It does not matter that Hamu has gone away,
if he does not come back again to fight against me.
But my cattle, which Hamu has carried off with
him, ought according to the law [1] to be restored by
the Whites—more especially as they were the cattle
which my father (Panda) gave me.'

About this time the Army was again called upon

statement, published at one time in colonial papers, that a
number of Hamu's wives and children had been massacred
by Zulus.

[1] Cetshwayo means the 'custom,' or compact, recognised
and acted on for some years past in Natal, of surrendering on
demand to the Zulu King the 'cattle' which might have been
carried off by male refugees, while their persons were protected.
At one time the Natal Government understood women and girls
to be included under the designation of 'cattle;' but, of late
years, under Sir H. Bulwer, the cattle given for them when
married, as *ukulobola*, have been handed over instead of the
persons of females.

to oppose the Whites. According to report the Zulus were to be sent to the coast.

All this while I continued still at the place which the King had assigned for me. Repeatedly, or almost every week, Cetshwayo sent to me to ascertain how I was getting on. One day two Zulus came to me saying 'We are come to you, having been sent by the King with the word that all your cattle, which are spread over the Zulu country, must be collected; for he fears lest they should be slaughtered by his people, since the Zulus are now so insolent and reckless that they have slaughtered even royal cattle; why then should they spare yours?' But I did not put much faith in all this, and, in order to see if it was true, I sent a Zulu whom I knew to the King to learn the truth of the matter. After five days he came back with two others of the King's people to get my cattle together, and take them to this place and that, under the name of 'royal' cattle. The Zulus who had brought the word to me previously, appeared to be wholly unknown to the King, and, no doubt, they wanted to get my cattle in this way into their own hands. The King, however, ordered that 'whoever had slaughtered one of the Whiteman's cattle should restore one of the same size '—which was done.

The Army of the Zulu King was called up at this time to the head kraal ' Nodwengu.' It was said that the Zulus were to be sent to the coast, to do battle with the soldiers; but they had first to be doctored by three Basutos. I only know or understand imperfectly in what that doctoring consisted. The Zulus, when they go to battle, are not allowed to make much noise, to go after girls, to discharge a fire-arm, or besmear with blood an assegai. If they abide faithfully by these conditions, the bullets of the Whites will slide off their skins, and they will gain the victory.

We were all under the impression that the Zulu Army had gone to the coast, when all at once the tidings spread that the Zulus had been defeated by the Whites at Kambula. On the day previous the disastrous conflict had taken place at the Hlobane Mountain, where the Whites had been cut off, and surrounded, by the Zulus. Here, indeed, the King's General, Umbilini, managed to get into his hands one Whiteman (Grandie) alive; but all the other whites were killed. This was not done by the King's Army, but by his northern battalions under the command of the aforesaid Umbilini (13). Next morning the entire Army of Cetshwayo arrived, which seems to have gone into fight without much consideration. As soon as they saw the tents of the Whites, each regiment of the King rushed to get at them as quickly as possible; from all quarters they flew at them. But the Whites too were ready, and received them with a rain of bullets. The Blacks, however, came nearer and nearer; but— what the Zulus had not expected—when they came to the place, there was a stone laager, and they found that the Whites had been too sharp for them, for they were too near to avoid it when they first got sight of it. Still the Zulus did not give up heart; they came at them through the gates; and some brought out of the fort blankets and iron pots, to show the King what they had done. About sundown the Zulus were put to flight, and, when they once began to run, there was no further resistance. But the darkness favoured them, for the Whites then returned to the fort. But for the laager which the Whites had made, they would very certainly have been killed by the Ngobamakosi, before the arrival of another Zulu regiment (14).

Next morning half the King's army was no longer visible; helped by the night they gave themselves only to flight, until they reached their kraals. Not more than a third of the army remained with

Mnyamana, Zibebu, and Maduna.[1] The Whites also seemed to have had enough of it, since they began to retire. When Mnyamana saw that the Whites had come forth out of the laager, he wished those remaining of the army to fight again, since the Whites had no more ammunition. But Zibebu would not hear of this, saying that 'it would be playing a dangerous game, since most of the Zulus had taken to flight.' So those Zulus who remained took their way back to the King.

I now heard an unusual amount of talk from the Zulus. Among other things they said that the

[1] 'The King and his full-brother Maduna are two of the finest men in the whole country. Cetshwayo is every inch of him a king, and whatever he says is to the point. The King's only son is still alive—about 9 or 10 years old, I believe.'—C. Vijn.

Cetshwayo's son, Dinuzulu, is older that Mr. Vijn supposes having been born before the great fight between Umbulazi and Cetshwayo in 1856; he must therefore now be about 23 years old, and he belonged to the Ngobamakosi regiment. But Cetshwayo has also an infant son, born to him by a daughter of Seketwayo. Cetshwayo's grandmother, the great wife of Senzangakona, was also alive at the beginning of the war. 'When the English force came, the Zulus begged her to quit her home and go away; but she refused, and when they urged it, she said that "she did not wish to live any longer and be troubled; for, when Chaka was killed by his brothers, she was left in charge of Dingani, and, when Dingani died, she was protected by Mpande, and Mpande left her to Cetshwayo, and now Cetshwayo, without having done any wrong, is being killed by the whitemen!" Thereupon the Inkosikazi (Queen) took a knife and cut her throat and died.'—Magema.

mounted red-coats were very much afraid, and quickly cried and ran away, whereas the mounted black-coats and foot-soldiers were generally not afraid of death, but fought on until they died revolver in hand.

Further the Zulus asked me 'what it meant that at the beginning of a battle so many white birds, such as they had never seen before, came flying over them from the side of the Whites? And why were they attacked also by dogs and apes, clothed and carrying fire-arms on their shoulders?' One of them even told me that he had seen four lions in the laager. They said, 'The Whites don't fight fairly; they bring animals to draw down destruction upon us.' Also, 'Why did the Whites cut off the heads of those who had fallen, and put them in their wagons? What did they do with these heads? Or was it to let the Queen see how they had fought?' [1]

When the King heard of the lost battle and of the many men who had fallen, he was exceedingly angry, and asked, 'Who had given the word for his people to be allowed to fight against Whites who

---

[1] There may be an allusion here to some regimental or private 'pets,' while the 'cutting off of heads' may refer to 'skulls,' which (it is well known) were carried off by some Whites from the battle-field.

had already entrenched themselves, since even in the open field one Whiteman was nearly as good as ten Zulus ?' The King was much grieved for the people who fell at the laager, many of whom belonged to the Ngobamakosi, his favourite regiment. For the King's plan had always been, whenever the Whites should have entrenched themselves, to make his army pass by them, in order thus to bring the Whites into the open field, or else to surround them from a distance, and make them die of hunger. But his people had not patience enough for all this ; and, each time they fought, they must go and rest again for two or three months before beginning another fight.

At this time Umbilini and Mnyamana came to the King with the White prisoner (Grandie) taken at Hlobane ; all this, however, I heard only by report. When they arrived, tobacco and gin (or rum) was supplied to the Whiteman by the King.[1] Further the King ordered that no harm should be done to this prisoner, but, at the end of the war, he

[1] 'The King was no drunkard ; though he drank a little gin, I never knew him to be the worse for liquor. I had seen the King on several previous occasions ; but during the war I was never in his presence until called to interpret Lord Chelmsford's letter.—C. Vijn.'

should return to the land of his own people. For
the present, however, he (Grandie) was to go back
with Umbilini, to build a kraal for him. Afterwards
Umbilini and (so it was said) Nkumbikazulu (brother
of Mehlokazulu) were killed, when engaged in steal-
ing horses (15). Then Grandie managed to escape,
although I don't believe his story (16); if he had
killed a Zulu, as he says, they would not have spared
me.

Now first I heard that the Zulus a few weeks
before had suffered a very severe blow on the coast,
whereby they had been put to flight and driven into
a flooded river, so that many lost their lives. Also
there were Tongas[1] in this force, who had had so
much of the war that they had returned straight to
their own land. What Cetshwayo said about this I
know not. I only know that the Zulus said that the
Whites had made a large, wide, round defence of
thorns. The general remark of the Zulus was,
'Why could not the Whites fight with us in the
open? But, if they are too much afraid to do this,
we have never fought with men who were so much
afraid of death as these. They are continually

[1] The Ama-Tonga (Tongas), an unwarlike people, living to
the N.E. of Zululand, and E. of Swaziland, were subject to the
Zulus.

making holes in the ground and mounds left open
with little holes to shoot through. The English
burrow in the ground like wild pigs. The Boers
are of more worth, who dare to come at once into
the open field.'

Much had I now to endure from the people;
above all they abused me. Then one said that ' he
would come stealthily upon me by night in order to
kill me '; while another said that ' he would bring
another Whiteman to me, and then I should have
company. Only I must not be afraid that any
harm would be done to me, since no one would dare
to venture upon that, through fear of the King; for
I was Cetshwayo's property, and would have now to
make fire-arms and cartridges for them.'

At this time, in the beginning of May, the girls
of the King's brother, who lived not far from me,
told me that, having taken beer to Ziwedu, they
had seen two Boers with the King at Maizekanye (17),
men with large hats and long beards; the King had
given them an ox on their arrival, and two oxen at
their departure. I asked what the Boers had done
with the King or had come to do. They told me
that the Boers had intended to join Cetshwayo with
all their people, to fight together with the Zulu
King against the English. Whether Cetshwayo

distrusted them I know not. He told them, however, that for the present he had no need of their assistance, but, in case he needed them, he would send for them. But then they must fight in front, since otherwise they might deceive the Zulus, and, instead of helping them, might fall upon their rear. 'No doubt,' said the King, 'the Boers are better than the English; for Panda was set up as King by the Boers, and died as King; whereas I, Cetshwayo, was crowned by the English, and, now that I have been King only a few years, my country is taken from me, and I, if they get hold of me, shall be killed or carried off to another land.'

A Zulu once told me that Kafirs had come from John Dunn, to ask if the King would agree that the Whites, since they were tired of fighting, should come and make payment with wagons and chests full of gold(18). Then said the King, 'Why have the Whites come to fight with me? They are in my land: I am not in their land. Let the Whites, therefore, go back with all their gold, which I don't desire. I desire nothing more than to remain King over my own land; that is all. Go back, therefore, and say that I do not want their gold; they might come with soldiers in the chests in place of gold.'

About the beginning of June two men came to

me with two horses, saying that 'I was to mount one of them, and we were to go to the King; for the King wished me to make haste and come to him, in order to translate for him the letters which had come from Natal.' This seemed all very pleasant and good ; but I did not place much confidence in the men who had come to me with the horses. However, go I must; there was nothing else to be done.

It was a rainy morning when we started. At every kraal we came to they had to supply us with food, and find also food for the horses, which was always done without a murmur. On the other side of the Black Imvolosi we decided to pass the night in one of the kraals ; we got there at 3 P.M., so that there was time enough to slaughter a beast, since we would gladly have something to eat. Also we were so lucky as to find there a good quantity of beer, which was very acceptable after a long ride on horseback.

As we went there were also numerous bodies of Zulus going to the King. At some places they were insolent towards me ; some pointed loaded guns at me, others made feints at me with their assegais ; but, for fear of the men sent by the King, they never went to extremes, and I got safely through,

though my heart more than once began to beat, and
I thought of my parents, brothers, and family, that
I should die without their ever coming to know
where and in what way I had perished. But thanks
to Cetshwayo! his word was as good as law, at least
as far as I was concerned.

Next morning we went on again. Our way was
through bush-country the whole day, and we saw
nothing but troops of Zulus going up continually to
the King. Some of them were amazed to see a
Whiteman in their midst; some or many of them
knew me, and said that 'I belonged to the King,
and the King had now sent for me to write letters
for the soldiers.' All were ready to believe that;
but some were only sorry that they could not, and
must not, wash their spears in my blood. An hour
before sundown we came out of the bush into the
open, and stayed to sleep at the first kraal we came
to. We did not get much to eat, there being
scarcity of food in the kraal.

Next morning the weather was quite different.
The morning-tide promised us a very pleasant day,
and we pressed on our way more vigorously to Umbonambi, one of the Royal Kraals, where the King
was at that moment. About 11 A.M. I rode into the
kraal, and in less than five minutes I had more

than a thousand Zulus about me, who pressed around me rather too closely ; but they were speedily dispersed by the headmen of the kraal, with a word that ' whoever dared to touch me would be killed by the King immediately, and, if he escaped, his family should suffer for him.' To this the Zulus replied ' Why did the King assure him that at a later time, when the war should be over, he should go again to Natal ? ' The headmen answered for the King that ' he never meant to keep me always as a captive ; his single object was that, by keeping me safe and taking good care of me, he might give proof to the Whites that Cetshwayo would not allow a White-man to be put to death for nothing, one who had come to him with good intentions, but was just like a White Chief, who also suffered no man, who had not deserved it, to be punished or put to death.'

The horses were now led away, and a hut was assigned to me, lying for my security between those of Mnyamana and Ziwedu. When I had washed, I was called by Mnyamana, who had got a pot of beer ready for me, thinking that I should perhaps be hungry. When I had partaken of my beer, a fine, nice piece of meat was brought to me, so that I was soon able to say that I was all alive again. Then he brought to me a letter which, as he informed me, had come about seven days ago. It was dated June 4, 1879, and was written by order of Lord Chelmsford, because the King had sent messengers to him asking for terms of peace, ' since quite enough men, white as well as black, had fallen in the war, and it was time now to make peace.' The letter was addressed by Col. Crealock to the White Trader, reported to be at Ulundi, with a request that I would translate it to the King. Its contents were very friendly and very simple ; all that Cetsh-wayo had to do, before the final terms of peace could be considered, was ' *to restore all that his soldiers had captured in the war with the Whites or, rather, had carried off*, ' all horses, oxen, arms, ammunition, and other property taken during the war ; ' though, on 'the representations of the messengers,' this demand was modified in a *post-scriptum*, dated June 5, to his giving up at once the oxen now with him, and the two 7-pounders, and promising to give up the arms and all the other things demanded, when collected(19).

The bearer of the letter said that Lord Chelms-ford would not burn Nodwengu, as it was Panda's kraal.

I translated the letter correctly for them, so that

they quickly understood it, and mastered its contents completely. My work was now done for this day.

Next day—as I suppose June 14—I was called to the King. I saluted him by simply taking off my hat before him, whereupon he greeted me saying that ' I was a good man, since I had not taken to flight, and had shown that I trusted him.' The King was sitting on a large roll of matting, with a handsome striped shawl on his shoulders, and a spear in his hand. He appeared friendly, but any-one observing him would see that he was sorrowful and had a presentiment of his approaching cala-mity.

Very soon he brought up political matters, and bade me take pencil and paper out of my bag, and write down at his dictation. When I was ready he began as follows—' Ask them how I can make peace when the Queen's Army is daily capturing my cattle, burning my kraals, and killing my people ? I be-lieve that, if they go out of my country, I shall make peace with them. But, if they go on doing what they are now doing, it will not be my fault if a calamity comes ; and then they will say, if White-men lose their lives, " It is all Cetshwayo's doing ! " whereas it is they who are doing it.' The King said also ' Say that Hulumente (Sir H. Bulwer),

Somtseu (Sir T. Shepstone), and Mr. John (Shepstone), who have brought on this war, should come to speak with me in order to bring the war to an end.'[1]

I now wished to have a reply to the letter of Lord Chelmsford; whereupon the King said that ' Of all that was there (at Isandhlwana) lost and destroyed, he had received very little; almost all had been carried off by his people to their kraals. What he had received was the oxen, though many of these had been slaughtered by his people before they came to him, and many had died afterwards of lung-sickness, so that only very few survived. But,' said the King, ' all this I did not take from the Whites out of their country; I merely defended myself in my own country, and overcame them there (at Isandhlwana), when, of course, my people took possession of all their goods.' So to Lord Chelmsford's letter he would give no reply, without first having another talk over it with his chief men.

[1] 'He seemed very dejected, and complained that he had been urged on too fast, that he had never objected [? refused to comply with] any of the terms of the ultimatum, but wished to discuss them further with H.E. the High Commissioner, and the Lieutenant-Governor; Somtseu too was to be present and everything was to be freely and fully discussed.'—*Statement of two Christian Natives,* reported by Col. Durnford, R.E., Jan. 8, 1879. [2242, p. 37.]

Thereupon my letter, written with lead-pencil, was sent off by four Zulus(20).

Every day there came large bodies of Zulus to the King, who got cattle from him to slaughter daily, but had also to bring corn out of their own gardens daily into the King's Kraal.

Seven or eight days afterwards we went with the King from Umbonambi to Umlambongwenya. I went with a headman ahead on horseback early in the morning, to seek out a hut for us in the Military Kraal. The King arrived two hours after us on foot, accompanied by all his people, who came singing after him. Before him went about twelve girls, who carried his blankets, mats, &c.

The King stayed here two nights only. From thence we went on to Umggikazi, where he ordered eight fine bullocks to be slaughtered. In two hours more he reached his Kraal 'Ulundi,' where he slaughtered the same evening ten more oxen. On the second day the four messengers came back who had been sent with my note, bringing it back again, and saying that ' they were not high enough persons to talk about Cetshwayo's country ; others therefore must come. But, if they came with empty hands, they might as well go back again, since Lord Chelmsford desired to have a strong proof that he

E

(Cetshwayo) was tired of the war.' The messengers
said that 'they were threatened that, if they came
back, they would be shot(21); and they were so
frightened at the reception they met with that they
brought back my note without delivering it.

Next morning therefore I had to write again
almost the same words, except that Cetshwayo sent
100 oxen and two or three elephants' tusks, with
the assurance that the two 7-pounders were on their
way.[1] Thereupon there came back a letter from
Lord Chelmsford to say that the King had not fulfilled what he was required to do ; but, inasmuch as
something had come, he (Lord Chelmsford) gave the
King still two days more, to fulfil the other con-
ditions(22).

Next morning there went off a letter from Cetshwayo with another appeal for peace(23); on the
outside of which I wrote in pencil, at the risk of my
life, a warning to Lord Chelmsford, telling him that
he must take care and be strong, since the King
had 20,000 men with him. And he sent also, as
a token of his sincerity, the sword of the Prince,
and 100 of his own white oxen, full-grown and fat,

---

[1] This letter, which was duly received by Lord Chelmsford,
was probably forwarded by him to the War Office. Mr. Vijn
only states from memory the substance of its contents.

which, when they had come to Nodwengu (about half a mile), were turned back(24) by force to Ulundi by his people, where they inveighed against him violently, and said that 'the cattle should never be given up to the Whites so long as they lived' (25).

Thereupon he made a powerful speech against his people, during which they stood before him perfectly mute, without saying a single word. His address was to this effect :—' In two battles you, my people, have gained the victory; in three or four others the Whites have gained it. After which of these battles did my people come back to me? After not one of them, whether gained or lost (26). No! At this moment the Whites are on all sides, west, south, east, and north. And, if to-morrow there should be another battle, you will all run away, and the Whites will follow and capture me only, and afterwards carry me away.' Then his people sware to Cetshwayo by the bones of their fathers, that, 'whether the day should be won or lost, they would come back to him.' Cetshwayo, it is plain, meant to save himself with these oxen, for he seemed to have a presentiment that he would lose the ensuing battle.

Towards evening there came down some wagons

and soldiers from Entonjaneni, and next morning the King went back from Ulundi to Umhlambong-wenya, I, of course, and his people going always with him. As soon as they reached the Kraal the King went with his people and formed a circle below—*i.e.* in front of—the Kraal. Then he sent half his people to bar the way on the side behind Nodwengu, and half on the side of Bulawayo, but with orders not to fire first upon the Whites. His intention was to guard against the Whites coming over the White Imvolosi.

On the day before the Battle of Ulundi there came a force of Whites on horseback over the White Imvolosi; but they were driven back with the loss of two or three men. The King was told that 15 Whites were killed.

Afterwards, in the afternoon of that day, the King went away—we knew not whither (27).

Next day at sunrise the Whites came over the river, and formed a square in front of Nodwengu. The battle began; I myself sat with some of the King's brothers and Great Chiefs upon a neighbouring hill to see the fight. About 9 A.M. the Zulus began to take to flight, and, once having shown their heels, they did not so easily come back again. Consequently we also took to flight; they would not let me go back, thinking that I might be of use tc them. Would it not also have been dangerous to meet full-butt the Blacks in their flight? Assuredly an end would have been made of me in that case.

After fleeing three miles in an open country we came into the bush. There was seen a sight indeed —women, old men, girls, children, cattle, and even wounded men from the battle among them! If Lord Chelmsford had pushed on after the fight, he would have captured them all, and the King also, and brought the war at once to an end.

Where the King was no one could tell us. We ourselves slept that night in the bush. After that we went, for eight or ten days together, from one place to another, without knowing where the King was. All the Zulus near the Black Imvolosi had left their kraals with their cattle and belongings; part went to the Bombo mountains, and part to the Ngome forest. The King gave orders for all the people to return with their cattle to their kraals at this time. He wished to collect four of his regiments, Ngobamakosi, Umcijo, Umbonambi, and Nokenke, to build a kraal for him, as his own were burnt. But this order was not carried out.

The troops captured at Ulundi two Zulus, who

had brought to the King a letter from Sir G. Wolseley addressed to Mnyamana, Tshingwayo, Seketwayo, Zibebu, telling them to come in with all the King's cattle and their guns, &c.(28). The King had sent for me to his hut, and told me to write a letter to Sir G. Wolseley and another to Mr. Fynney (Border Agent). I had to tell Sir G. Wolseley that Hayana, brother of Zibebu, Mzilikazi, Vumandaba, Mavumengwana, Sintwangu, and another, were sent to say that 'the King was getting his cattle together to send in, but they must give him time, as they were scattered all over the country, and his people were killing them one after another—that the English should take pity on him and leave to him the country of his father.' I was to say to Mr. Fynney that, 'if he would say a good word for him to the Government, he would be paid well with a good herd of oxen.' I know that the letters were delivered; but I saw no more of the messengers who took them, and who were captured by the troops at Ulundi, nor do I know the result.

Mnyamana, Tschingwayo, &c. did come in with some of the King's cattle; but they were detained, and were sent to a small kraal, Esindeni near Ulundi(29). Also three of the King's brothers,

Ziwedu,[1] Sukane, and Mgidhlana, came in soon afterwards to surrender, but were not allowed to go away. They were afraid that the Swazis, with whom they were threatened by Sir G. Wolseley, would come and kill their women and children, and were told that they must send out their people to bring in the King, and that they would not be released till he was caught. Ziwedu told me this. In fact, even after the Battle of Ulundi the Zulus treated me very well.

At last we found the King in one of Mnyamana's kraals, not far from the Ngome forest. While I was with the King at this kraal, I had a talk with him in which he asked ' What did the English want him to do?' I said 'I did not know certainly; but I supposed that they were angry because he had turned out the Missionaries(30). He said ' Well! the Missionaries were very troublesome; they wanted to be King over me, and, when I wished to talk with the Governor of Natal, they came and told me that I must do so and so, as if they were kings in the land, whereas it was not their country, but mine.' As to the marrying of the young men

---

[1] ' Ziwedu ' is not mentioned in the Official Notice (Note 29) as having surrendered ; in fact, he ' came in ' the day afterwards (Aug. 16) and was 'detained.'

he said that 'he was quite willing to let all the regiments marry, except the three youngest.' He said also that 'he was willing to give the English all the country on this (the Natal) side of the Umhlatuze ; but, if they divided it at the White Imvolosi, they would take away the whole country.'

After staying there fourteen days he went back and remained ten days in Ziwedu's kraal in the land of Nongome. While there he received more than one notice that he must come himself to the Whites. Also I did my best to persuade him in that direction ; but, being made afraid by others, he dared not venture to come in, lest he should be shot dead or carried over the sea to Robben Island.[1]

When he heard that the troops from England had again come back into Zululand, he asked himself the question ' What to do now ? '—since he had heard from a Kafir sent by Mr. Dunn that ' the Whites had not come back of their own accord, but had been brought back by the coast Zulus, who said that Cetshwayo had again collected other troops

---

[1] Of course Cetshwayo knew the story of Langalibalele. But he had also (Note 29) been warned by Dabulamanzi that this would be his fate, if he surrendered, and he had probably heard the same from others, white or black, before the war began.

and was up in arms, and so the English forces came
back again.'

The King has complained much about John
Dunn, ' who,' said he, ' has enjoyed so much from
me, and who was as good as King, on which account
he has now come to fight against me, in order to
kill me and be King alone.'

The Zulus also told me that John Dunn had
sent to say that ' he was buying up all the King's
cattle for him, but his money was at an end, and he
could not buy any more.'

After the Battle of Ulundi 600 or 700 of the
King's oxen were sold to Dunn and Woodhouse
(butcher) privately, not by auction, for 2*l*. a head,
each well worth 5*l*. in Natal, and splendid King's
white oxen, worth 20*l*. each in Natal, most of them
inoculated, were sold to the same men for 10*l*. each.[1]

One of the King's brothers told me that, if it
came to ' talking over ' the matter with the English
Chiefs, as Cetshwayo so often desired, John Dunn
would get into a scrape with the Whitemen.   For
Cetshwayo himself did not want to get guns until

---

[1] From a perfectly independent and trustworthy source it
appears that such private sales took place more than once, at
prices ridiculously low compared with those which might have
been obtained in open market.

John Dunn told him that, 'if he did not, he would
be a fool, and be a child in the eyes of other nations,
and they would invade his country and take away
his cattle.   So he bought the guns—chiefly from
John Dunn himself.'   In fact, Mr. John Dunn has
introduced many thousands of guns into Zululand,
which cost him 10s. 6d. each, and each of which he
sold at first for ten head of cattle, which gradually
dropped to one head; and finally, when other traders
brought in the same guns, he tried to keep them
out by selling two or three guns for a beast.   In
fact Mr. Dunn has made a very large fortune by the
King, against whom he has now been fighting.

Well! on a certain day the King told me to go
to Sir G. Wolseley and tell him that 'he (Cetshwayo)
had no more army, and was employed in collecting
his cattle to hand them over to the Whites.'   When
I brought this message to Sir G. Wolseley he asked
me to go by myself and find the King and persuade
him to surrender.   Being a Dutchman and having
been in close intimacy with the King, I was afraid
of the consequences of refusing to do his bidding
and I undertook the task.   But I said, 'He will have
gone away from the place where I left him, and I
don't know where he is now.'   Sir G. Wolseley then
offered me a bribe of 200l., and promised to keep

the matter of this payment secret; he told me to go
to-morrow before sunrise; he would give me three
days to bring him in; but, if I managed it in two
days, he would give me 50*l.* more.

Accordingly next morning I started early from
Ulundi, and before sundown I reached the place
where I had left the King. Here I offsaddled for an
hour and took food, and at sundown saddled-up,
having made enquiries, but not having got any information, except as to the direction in which the
King had gone. I set out for the kraal of Ziwedu,
the King's brother, which I reached about 10 P.M.,
when it was dark. I off-saddled and went into his
hut, where I found him and several other brothers
of the King and other headmen. He asked me
what I had done. I said that 'I had told Sir G.
Wolseley that the King had no *Impi*, and was quite
alone, and was collecting his cattle to give them up.'
They asked what Sir G. Wolseley said about that.
I said that 'Sir G. Wolseley had sent me with a
message to the King and his brothers. I must tell
his brothers that they must surrender and bring in
guns and royal cattle, and, if they would do well,
they must try to persuade the King to come in, and,
if he would not, they must take him by force, and
bring him in. And I must tell the King that he

was no longer king, that, if he surrendered, he would
be treated well, no harm would be done to him, and
his life would be spared, but all his cattle belonged
to Sir G. Wolseley.' Then I told Ziwedu to send
the others out of the hut, and when they were gone
I asked him to tell me where the King was. At
first he said that he did not know; but I said 'I
must see him and speak with him.' He then told
me I could sleep now, and in the morning he would
give me men who would bring me where the King
was.

Next morning I saddled-up and started with one
native guide to bring me to the King, and after ten
miles came where he was on the Mona River. I went
to the King's hut; he called me in and allowed no
one else to enter, so that we were alone. He greeted
me and asked me what I had done. I said, as before, that I had told Sir G. Wolseley he (the King)
had no *Impi* and was collecting his cattle for surrender. He asked anxiously what Sir G. Wolseley
had said, and I told him that Sir Garnet had said
that he was no longer King, aud never should be
again, that he must surrender, and his life should be
spared, if he came in of his own accord.' He asked
me what kind of man the Great Chief was. I described him as well as I could. But the King said

'That is not the Great Chief, because he is not travelling with Dunn, as this one is, and he is very tall; and the one who is travelling with Fynney and this one travelling with Dunn are two deceivers, who are trying to get my land.' In fact he was greatly confused to know who was really the Great Chief, as there appeared to be so many who claimed to be so.[1]

I tried hard to get him to go with me to Sir G. Wolseley; but he said 'It was not safe for him to do so; so soon as he appeared he would be shot.' I said that he might trust me that he would not be shot. But he would not go, saying that 'he could not believe the English, he could not depend on them; they play crafty tricks (*ba namacebo*)'(31); and he bade me go back that same day and see the Great White Chief. He also said that 'the White people ought to leave his country, taking all his cattle and all the guns, and leave him in peace with his people, to dig the land and get food.' At that

[1] Sir B. Frere, Lord Chelmsford, Sir G. Wolseley, Sir H. Bulwer, had each been called 'the Great Chief.' At one time also, no doubt, Sir T. Shepstone, who had installed Cetshwayo, and had been received with the royal salute 'Bayete!' was 'the Great Chief' for the Zulus. But Mr. Vijn says, 'At the Blood River Meeting with the Zulu Indunas Sir T. Shepstone was angry because Mnyamana called him by his name "Somtseu," and said that he was only an Induna like himself.'

time the Zulus would have given up all their guns at the King's command.

I went away on my return and came to Ziwedu's, to get another horse. He asked me what the King had said; I told him he was afraid to come in. Ziwedu wanted to go with me to Sir G. Wolseley, together with his brothers Sukana and Gidhlana, but did not like to do so without the King's knowledge. So I went away, slept in the bush, and reached Sir G. Wolseley on the third day, going right into the camp. They asked what I wanted, and one went to Sir G. Wolseley, who came to meet me, and told me to go to Dunn's wagons (half-a-mile off) and he would come directly. He came very shortly after me, and asked me if I had found the King. I said that 'the King was afraid to come, but his brothers were coming.' He told Dunn to give me food, and said that we were to start at 3 P.M. with 500 mounted men under Major Barrow to capture the King, I and E. Thring going in front as guides.

We started as ordered, and went on till sundown. When we were going down the Emahlabatini, about ten or twelve miles from Ulundi, having been about two hours on the road, it was very steep, and all dismounted, except myself, being lame.

But it soon became very dark, and the country

was thick with bush, and, though we were on the wagon-road, it was impossible to see the track, the grass being as high as a man. Just as it became dark, twelve shots were fired in the bush, the sounds coming from different quarters. We could not imagine what they meant; but the troops thought that the King's Army was in the bush, and that they would be presently surrounded. I assured them that there was no Impi. Then they found out that one of the soldiers was lost, and that this was the cause of the firing, and they fired twenty-five shots themselves. We then went on with eight or ten lighted lamps, very judiciously giving notice of our coming. Twice we missed our road and so lost from two to three hours. At last we came out of the thick part of the bush, and E. Thring went to a kraal well known to him, where he got two natives as guides. We now went on very well to the Black Imvolosi, which we reached about midnight, and then stopped an hour, without off-saddling, lighted fires and cooked some coffee, and started again about 1 A.M. Between 1 and 5 A.M. we only went $2\frac{1}{2}$ miles; it was always 'halt! halt! halt!' I told Major Barrow that, if we went on at this rate, it would be impossible to reach the King's place before 8 A.M. (whereas I had expected to get there by 5 A.M.). Major Barrow said it was impossible to go any quicker, as they could not leave behind any stragglers for fear of an Impi. We changed guides at the first kraal we came to, and went on and reached the top of the Nongome ridge about an hour after sunrise, the men having all dismounted for the ascent, and I also, though lame, as the horses were tired.

On the top of the ridge Major Barrow wished me to point out the place where the King was. I pointed out the direction in which it lay, but could not see the place itself. He asked how many miles further it was. I said 'About ten miles.' He did not like that, being, I suppose, tired and sleepy. When we came near Ziwedu's kraal Major Barrow asked me whose kraal it was. I told him it belonged to Ziwedu, one of the King's brothers. Major Barrow proposed to seize him, and tie him up, to make him tell where the King was. I did not agree to this, as he had always treated me very well. So we passed by. At every kraal natives brought guns and assegais, wishing to surrender, but were told to take them to Sir G. Wolseley at Ulundi. We descended a steep hill, crossed a little spruit, and then climbed up another steep hill, where the soil was of red clay and slippery with dew. All dismounted again here, and had great difficulty in getting up.

When we reached the top it was now about 11 A.M., and we halted for an hour, without off-saddling. Major Barrow asked how many miles further it was now. I said 'About six miles, I supposed.' We went on about four miles, and I then pointed out the spot, though the kraal itself was not visible. Major Barrow asked how many miles further it was, as we had come four miles, and it seemed to him a long way off yet. I said 'I do not understand English miles, not being an Englishman'—four English miles make about one Dutch mile—'I had only gone this way once, and had not measured the distance.' Major Barrow said 'I don't believe you know where you left the King. I think you are misleading me.' I then said 'If I told you six miles before and we have gone four miles, you should know that there are two more without asking me.' Major Barrow said 'You must know that I am in command of these troops and you are under me.' I said 'I am not a soldier, but a private individual.' He again demanded the distance to the kraal where the King was. I then said 'I did not know or, rather, I could not tell him.' He told me to point out the direction. I said 'I think it is that way' (pointing). He said 'You only think; you don't know.' I replied 'I think that is the right direction—two hills up and two hills down.' After that he was angry with me and disliked me.

A quarter of an hour afterwards we reached the kraal where I had left the King, which seemed empty and deserted. The troops rode up and surrounded it; it was now about 1 P.M. At last three Zulus appeared, one of whom said that the King had left in the afternoon of the day previous, and pointed out in what direction he had gone. 'The King,' he said, 'had gone to a kraal in a valley by the Mona River about a mile away.' This river runs between very high, steep, and stony hills, between which are lateral ravines covered with bush.

We off-saddled here for three hours, and the troop was divided, half the men remaining, the other half advancing with picked horses. I saw no more of those who remained behind; but I believe that they stayed there three or four days. We went on to the kraal where the King had slept the night before, and heard that he had killed a beast there the very morning on which we arrived. As soon as we had topped the Nongome ridge, he was informed that troops were coming, and went away no one knew whither. A Zulu told us that he had gone to Mbopa's country (Kwa' Hlabisa). After many difficulties in crossing rivers and mounting hills we

reached Mbopa's kraal. On topping the hill just
before reaching the kraal we saw the flash and heard
the report of a gun a long way off, which was meant,
I think, as a signal for Cetshwayo. We off-saddled
close to the kraal, the horses being tied in a square
on the outer sides of which we lay. We asked
Mbopa and his men to tell us whither the King had
gone; but they either could not, or would not, tell
us.

Next morning at sunrise we saddled-up, taking
possession of Mbopa and his men, and went on to
the kraal of his son Nkabanina. On arrival we
found the kraal deserted by its inhabitants, but full
of royal cattle, some of which we seized for food; I
don't know what became of the rest. We off-saddled
and sent out scouts, who by noon had collected forty
Zulus. I did not know at the time that Lord
Gifford had gone on with part of the force to three
other kraals of Nkabanina. Major Barrow required
the forty Zulus to tell whither the King had gone,
and said that he would shoot one of them if they
did not tell him. They could not, or would not, tell
him. At this time one of Jantje's mounted natives
came with the news that they had caught one of the
King's horses and three of his followers; but, on one
of the latter running away, the other two were sent

after him, and all three disappeared together. We
then went after Lord Gifford, came up with him
about 4 P.M., off-saddled, and slept at two kraals of
Nkabanina.

Here Major Barrow and Lord Gifford tried to
get information from the people as to Cetshwayo's
whereabouts. All the huts were plundered of their
little valuables, and the stores of grain were taken
for the horses, but without success. Among the
Zulus here I recognised an old man, one of the
King's household-officers. The people told us to
ask him, as he had left the King that morning. He
stated that, 'though this was true, he knew nothing
about his hiding-place now.' At last, about 8 P.M.,
he agreed to show us next morning the direction in
which the King had gone.

We saddled-up at sunrise, the troop being again
subdivided into two parties, each with four Zulu
guides to trace the footsteps of the King. At first
our progress was difficult, owing to the thickness of
the bush. We found many spoors, but could not
make much of them. At 9 A.M. we met again, and
went on together, following a spoor which we
thought was the right one, as we saw a broken pot
that had contained beer, which had probably been
used by the King. But we lost the spoor on the

north side of the Black Imvolosi. A few men crossed the river which was here wide and low, but bad through quicksands. Three men, with their horses, were spilled and rolled over in them, and could not cross. We were now about twenty in number, Major Barrow and Lord Gifford being with us. We fell in with a Zulu who told us that he had been sent by Mnyamana to tell the people to surrender their guns, and he was allowed to go. He said that he had heard at a kraal of Somkele, three miles further on, that the King had been there. Lord Gifford went on with a few men to that kraal. I wished to follow, but Major Barrow would not allow me to go, as I was riding his favourite horse which was tired, and said that I must go back with him across the Black Imvolosi. I did not, however, cross the river, but remained with three mounted Natives whom I found there. Major Barrow with a few men rejoined those who had been left on the other side of the river.

Half-an-hour before sundown two mounted men arrived, who had been sent back by Lord Gifford to Major Barrow to say that Lord Gifford had information about the King, and would go on in pursuit. We then started to follow Lord Gifford, but, it being dark, we missed our way, and were unable to find him and his party. At daylight we went on, but could not overtake them. Lord Gifford had gone on to Emkandhlwini, a Military Kraal on the coast. An officer (Capt. Nourse, I believe) with ten or fifteen men went to seek information at a kraal at a junction of the White Imvolosis. Major Barrow told off four guides to await his return, and then started for Ulundi with the remainder of the force. I remained with the four guides. Thring told me that Major Barrow wished me to go to Ulundi. I said that I did not wish to go. Afterwards, two mounted men, sent by Major Barrow, came to know why I did not join him, as I was not allowed to go with Lord Gifford. So I went with Major Barrow to Ulundi. After I had joined him, about two miles from where the four guides were left, Major Barrow collected all the food he could spare, and sent Jantje and some of his men to take it to Lord Gifford.

That night we slept at Maizekanye, which had been fired by the Zulus, as had been ten of the thirteen Military Kraals near Ulundi, including Ulundi itself. There were twenty-seven Military Kraals altogether. I wished to go on to Ulundi, but was not allowed to do so, because the horse which I rode (Major Barrow's) was tired.

Next morning we started for the camp at Ulundi.
When we had passed Umbonambi, we met a detachment of foot-soldiers with John Dunn's wagon-
driver as guide. They were searching for goods
hidden away in caves. Major Barrow went to the
camp, and I to John Dunn's wagon, where I slept,
sending back Major Barrow's horse to the camp.

Next day John Dunn went early to the camp,
and on his return said that I had better go to Sir
G. Wolseley and tell him all about the matter, as
Major Barrow laid all the blame of failure on my
shoulders, saying that ' I had taken him by a road
twenty miles longer than was necessary.' I went to
Sir G. Wolseley about 8 A.M. He came out of his
tent, and I told him that the fault was not mine, as
he had sent too many men with me, who could not
travel fast enough, and made too much noise, firing
guns and displaying lanterns.' I said 'if he had
given me fifty Natal Volunteers, the King would have
been in his hands before now.' He said ' Why the
devil did you not tell me that before ? ' I reminded
him that ' I had told him that I only required fifty
men; but perhaps he did not remember that. And
I could not tell, when we started, that five hundred
men would go so slowly.' Sir G. Wolseley said
' You took them by a wrong road, and up and down

steep hills, where the men had to dismount.' I said ' I did not make the country myself; it is as it is. I took them the same way I had gone before.' He said ' I am sorry,' and I said ' So am I,' and he ' But you are not so sorry as I am. However, go your way, and I will send you a little present.'

Dunn told me that, when Major Barrow came up, Sir G. Wolseley said to him ' Why have you come back ? You are not the man who ought to have come back. If you had been out for ten months, you ought not to have come back without the King.' A party was sent out again that very morning before 8 A.M., to follow up the pursuit of the King. But they did nothing but capture King's cattle, and burn kraals, and plunder all the huts of curiosities. I have seen a soldier with four milking-bowls over his shoulders, two in front and two behind, four or five girls' bead-fringes round his waist, three men's tail-pieces slung over one shoulder and below the other, like a shawl, a number of bangles on his wrists, on his hat a Zulu's ball of feathers, four or five assegais in one hand and six or seven knobkirries in the other. Many of the officers also wore copper and brass bangles as the spoils of war.

In the evening I received from Dunn ten sove

reigns for my trouble from Sir G. Wolseley through Sir P. Colley.

Next day I got a note offering me the post of interpreter at 1*l.* a day, and, as I was doing nothing, I agreed to the proposal.

Next day I was sent out under a staff officer (whose name I forget) with twenty-five men. We went through the bush over the Black Imvolosi, and slept not far from Zibebu's Kraal. I do not know what particular object we had in view.

Next day we went as far as the first kraal belonging to Zibebu, where we offsaddled. We found here some guns which we smashed, but no Martini-Henrys. Then we made the owners of the kraal give up their stored mealies for our horses, which they did very unwillingly, being afraid of starvation, and one actually cried, saying that ' they would have nothing now to eat.' The officer took only half the mealies from that kraal, and took the rest from another kraal. He then sent for the headman of this second kraal, and sent him with a message to Zibebu that he must surrender, and bring in his guns and royal cattle, and if he did not come in two days' time, they would come and burn all the kraals in his country and take all his cattle. At 2 P.M. we saddled-up again and started on our return to Ulundi, but slept not far from the Black Imvolosi.

Next morning we saddled-up and reached Ulundi safely. That same day a large force was sent out, horse and foot and natives, to the Black Imvolosi wagon-drift, to prevent the King passing there. Troops were spread at this time in every direction over the country.

Next day I stayed at Dunn's wagon, who was out with the force, but separate from them.

Next day Dunn and I, while at supper, received a summons from Sir G. Wolseley to come at once to him. When we arrived Sir P. Colley told me that 'I was wanted to go on an expedition that night; he had a good horse for me, and our party would be about twenty-four Whitemen and sixty Natives on foot, with two Zulu guides, who had brought information that a sick Zulu had seen two *ingcekus* (household-officers) of the King with the Umtunzi (King's shadow, meaning the King himself), and we were to go and capture the King.'

We started and went all right till midnight; but then we came to the bush, and we had to go down a very stony hill, where they all had to dismount except myself. I was in front with one of the guides, the other being with the Natives in the

rear. And every now and then a cry was heard
'Where is the guide? Where is the interpeter?
They go too fast.' When we had got down the hill,
the officer in charge said 'I was to tell the guide
not to take them by such bad roads, by which it
was impossible to go, and I was to ask him how
many miles further we had to go.' I told the officer
that 'the Zulu could not tell him anything about
miles;' but I could not make him understand this.

Now we went on through bush and stony places,
sometimes dismounting, sometimes halting to pick
our hats up (I lost my hat three times). We
crossed the Black Imvolosi about an hour before
daybreak, and came to the place where the King
and his two servants had been seen. We surrounded
four kraals there, but did not find any trace of the
King, although he had been there three days before
and had killed a beast there.

We now killed a beast and tried to get information as to the direction in which the King had gone.
They pointed out where the King was. But the
officer said that, 'inasmuch as we had neither blankets nor food, and the King was three days ahead,
it would be impossible to follow him up.' So we
returned to Ulundi. And, although I wished to
follow the King with the Natives, I did not mention

my wish, because previously Major Barrow had not allowed me to follow up Lord Gifford. We came upon the other troops stationed at the wagon-drift of the Black Imvolosi, where we off-saddled, and had food, and at 4 P.M. set off again for Ulundi.

My road to Dunn's wagon branched off about two or three miles from Ulundi, and I wished to go on to the wagon with the horse I was riding. But I was not allowed to do so, and was told that I must go on with the horse to the camp, which I did not like to do. So I had to dismount and proceed to the wagon on foot, and got there about an hour after midnight.

Two days afterwards I went to the place where my wagon and oxen were, and made ready to start for Natal. The day on which I got it ready the news reached us that the King was caught at a kraal on the Ibululwana, a small stream which runs into the Isikwebesi, where the country is open, on the border of the Ngome forest (32).

Next morning I started with my wagon and oxen, and seventy head of cattle I had left,[1] and went on to Ulundi, having to pass it on my

---

[1] It appears that these cattle, the produce of his sales of goods in the early part of his trip, together with his wagon and oxen, were kept safely for Mr. Vijn under the King's protection.

way to Natal. When I got to Ulundi the King was now in front of me about seven miles, having reached Ulundi the day before I did, so that I had no opportunity of seeing him, as he was gone before I arrived. When the King was captured, about 4,000 head of cattle taken from the Zulus was restored to them.

I now went to Mr. John Shepstone and stated my claims for compensation from Zibebu for two hundred head of cattle, either stolen from me by his people—probably under his orders, for he bears a bad name—or destroyed by disease which they had caught in his kraal, also for three guns stolen at the same time, and for the murder of my two men. Mr. John Shepstone said that he had nothing to do with it, being only here as interpreter, and ' I must go to Sir G. Wolseley.' So I went to Sir P. Colley, and he told me to set my claim down on paper, and he would lay it before Sir G. Wolseley. I did so, and the same day in another paper I represented my claim for the 250*l.* promised me by Sir G. Wolseley, as I had done my work in two days and a half. Having delivered these letters I went away to John Dunn's wagon, and came back in the afternoon, when I was told to go to Sir G. Wolseley's secretary, who said that Sir Garnet would not allow me the 250*l.*, because the King had not been caught through me ; [1] but he would give me 50*l.*' So I was paid 40*l.* more. As to the claims against Zibebu he said that ' he (Sir G. W.) could do nothing ; even if they had killed me, the murderers could not have been punished, because it was their own country, and we traders went in at our own risk.'

I went back to Dunn's wagon and there I met Zibebu, and I asked him for ten head of cattle he owed me for goods obtained on a previous trip. He said ' he had no old debts now ; the war had cleared off everything, and he would not pay me.' Of course he had just been made one of the thirteen petty Kings in Zululand, together with John Dunn, Mlandela, Somkele, Mgotshane, Hamu, Seketwayo, Mgitsho, Mfanawendhlela, Gaozi, and three others, whose names I do not know. The Zulus told me that, when Hamu left to join the English, he said that he should be made King of the country, and they asked me how it was possible that he should be made King by the English, when he was much more bloodthirsty than Cetshwayo, and had killed

---

[1] It would seem that the troops were put upon the right scent by Mr. Vijn, who took them to the place where he had left the King, from which they tracked him to his last retreat.

through his doings many more men than Cetshwayo, for it was he that gave the order to the Tulwana regiment at the Umkosi (Feast of Firstfruits), January, 1878, to attack the Ngobamakosi, who were disliked as the King's favourite regiment, and who had nothing but stakes to fight with, whereas the Tulwana went and got their assegais out of their huts nigh by. The King blamed him for that, and Hamu, not liking the reproof, went away (33).

After that I went home to Natal. I am now going to trade in Swaziland, as under the present system it is impossible to trade in Zululand. How can a man trade there, when he has to make arrangements with each Chief, and John Dunn alone demands 25*l*. from everyone who wishes to trade in his territory, even though he has but a single wagon.

It is equally impossible, in my judgment, that the present 'settlement' of Zululand should last. The Zulus are certain to fight among themselves, and there is no central Government to restrain them. I believe that, if Cetshwayo were brought back and set to rule the country under the supervision of a Resident, it would be far better governed for the good of all parties than it can possibly be

under the present arrangement. I believe that the
Zulus would be glad to see him back again, the
army being broken up, and the young men left free
to marry. And Cetshwayo, after this terrible war,
would, I am convinced, readily agree to all this, or
he would even be glad to have allowed him in his
father's land a place where he might live as a
private individual.   C. VIJN.

P.S.—During my four years' experience I never
heard that the King was killing many people, nor
do I believe that he has killed to anything like the
extent with which he has been credited. My belief
is that the statements made in 1877 to the Natal
Government [1883, p. 2] by two of Mr. Oftebro's
converts, that 100 people had been butchered in
one day, shot with guns, not killed with assegais,
and that the Zulu People, great and small, were
tired of the rule of Cetshwayo, are absolutely false.
I have been in the country three-quarters of the
whole time since October, 1874, and I never heard
anything of the kind. As to the killing of girls in
1876 it is utterly impossible that *many* girls were
killed(34). I deny emphatically, and totally disbelieve, that Cetshwayo was a bloodthirsty tyrant ;
though he had, of course, to enforce from time to

time the laws of his country, and, if he had not done so, where should I have been, who owed my safety to the order maintained by the King?

I remember distinctly two cases of killing which came under my notice. In one case a man had committed adultery with one of the King's women, and, on confessing his fault, he was pardoned. On a second offence, which he also confessed, he was put to death. In the other case a man, Umkogwana, was charged with witchcraft, and said he knew that he was brought up to the King as an *umtagati*. John Dunn, who was present, said 'then he must be an *umtagati*, else he would not know why he was brought up.' Umkogwana said ' I am not an *umtagati*, but there (pointing to Dunn) is the snake who will kill you and be King over your land.'

I heard the above from trustworthy Zulus, and they are the only two cases of which I have certain knowledge. I have heard of other cases, where men have been brought up as *umtagatis*, and not killed. In fact, it was not the King who killed in most cases, but the jealousy or superstition of their own people.—C. V.

NOTES

BY THE BISHOP OF NATAL.

Note 1, *page* 3.

'I found that there were all sorts of wild rumours going about from station to station (in Zululand), one that *the British Government intended to annex Zululand at once* (1877). I am afraid that this and the like rumours have done harm. Several of the missionaries have been frequently to the King of late, and, as he has told me, have worried him to such an extent that he does not want to see them any more.'—Mr. Fynney, July 4, 1877 [*Blue Book*, 1961, p. 47].

'I observe that an impression prevails in Zululand to the effect that the country is likely to be annexed to the British dominions at an early date. I should much regret to see this belief gain ground either in Zululand or in any of the neighbouring countries.'—Lord Carnarvon, Aug. 31, 1877 [1961, p. 60].

Note 2, page 6.

'I found the Zulu King in a very excited state to-day. He said that rumours had reached him from Natal that the Natal Government had taken steps to completely surround him, and that their intention was, if they could, to seize Cetshwayo, as a message had come from the Queen across the water to ask if it was true that Cetshwayo had said that he was equal to Her Majesty, and, if so, he was to be bound and brought to confront her, and that I was only blinding him as to the movements of the Natal Government, and that he intends taking steps to *protect himself*, as he could not be taken as a child. He is quite correct about the reports which reach him as regards the movements on the Natal side, raised, I am sure, by a lot of inconsiderate Whites, for the sake of mischief.'—Mr. John Dunn, Oct. 10, 1878 [2260, p. 53].

'Three Zulu messengers, sent to me by the King, just arrived, inform me that the Zulus are all arming by order of the King.

'It would appear that some one has informed the King that the Natal Government intends to invade Zululand with the purpose of taking him, and that the arming of the Zulus is a precautionary measure.'—Mr. Fynney, Oct. 24, 1878 [2260, p. 55].

Note 3, page 8.

The Zulus supposed that the *northern* column (Col. Wood's), as it came from the direction of the

Transvaal, had been sent by Somtseu (Sir T. Shepstone), and accordingly they spoke of it as 'Somtseu's *Impi.*' This idea was, no doubt, confirmed in their minds by the fact of its including a Volunteer Mounted Force of Border Boers under Piet Uys.

The allusion here made by the Zulus to 'the Boers being on their way to fight with them in their own land' probably refers to this column, and especially to the fact that about the middle of October, 1878, Col. Wood 'sent from Utrecht a detachment of troops to Lüneberg' [2260, p. 46], in the district north of the Pongolo claimed by the Zulus—and apparently not without reason—as part of their territory which the Boers had 'annexed,' as well as that south of the Pongolo, which the Commissioners declared to belong to the Zulus, and which was actually given to them by Sir B. Frere, but a considerable portion of which has since, for reasons of policy, been again 'annexed' by Sir G. Wolseley and given to the Transvaal under English rule.[1]

Accordingly Mr. Dunn says [2260, p. 54], 'One report is that *a large troop of mounted men have gone to take possession of the disputed land on the Pongolo,* where the kraal was built.'

[1] 'The *Transvaal Argus* has reason to believe that the new boundary-line between Zululand and the Transvaal will remove many of the heart-burnings which existed among some of the farmers living in the disputed territory.'—*Natal Colonist,* Oct. 9, 1879.

Sir Garnet Wolseley has stated that the tract of land he has re-annexed includes all the farms—which, according to the Commissioners, had been eaten out of Zululand—except two.—*Official Statement.*

And on Nov. 10, 1878, he writes in the King's name [2308, p. 16], 'Cetshwayo states that he thanks H.E. for the message brought by Umgwazi, and states that the reason of his calling his men up was on account of hearing the reports brought to him about *an armed body of men being sent to the Transvaal Border,* and the reason for his sending to Mr. Fynney and Mr. Jackson was on his hearing that there was an armed force to be sent into the Zulu country to seize him.

' Cetshwayo hereby swears, in presence of Mnyamana, Hamu, Ntshingwayo, and all his other Chiefs, that he has no intention or wish to quarrel with the English.'

Note 4, page 8.

'Chaka was assassinated on Sept. 23, 1828, by his brothers (Dingane and Mhlangana), at his residence, "Dukuza," in this colony (on the Lower Umvoti); and he lies buried where he was killed in one of the *erven* of the newly laid-out town called "Stanger." '—Sir T. Shepstone [1137, p. 4].

The grave of Chaka has not been disturbed, nor rifled of its contents by sacrilegious hands, as that of our faithful ally and friend, the late King (Panda), Mpande, has been at the end of the war, to add another disgrace to the English name.

' We were going with some soldiers and natives under Col. ——; there were 400 soldiers and 180 natives. In the morning the Colonel and officers asked John Dunn—" Where is the grave of Mpande?" He pointed with his hand and showed where it was—a long way off. We started after breakfast, and got there about noon. The soldiers took with them four spades and a pick. John Dunn went with us, and pointed out the place again when we came to it. Mpande's grave was in the middle, fenced in with stakes, and with other graves around it. It was in the midst of a thicket of bush; but some of the trees had been burnt last year by a grass-fire. The soldiers first pulled up the stakes and made fires with them to cook their food. Then came two soldiers with spades, and another with a pick, together with Col. —— and Mr. ——. They dug up the King's grave, and came first upon some stones and wicker-work, and then they took out his bones wrapped in his blankets. I stood near enough (about ten or fifteen yards off, as indicated) to see that there had been four blankets of different colours wrapped round the body, one inside the other, and outside there had been a kaross made of jackal-skins; but this last was quite rotten, and three of the blankets also were much decayed, though one seemed to be sound and held together. The white men were surprised and said, "How is it that the blankets have lasted so long (seven years)?" The black people asked our captain, "What are you doing, digging up a man's bones?" Said he, "We are doing it in order to catch the King; for, now that we have dug up his father, we shall soon catch him." So they took out all his bones, a soldier belonging to the hospital handling them, and I saw the bones of the King, and the skull with the teeth, and the leg-bones—they took them all, and put them into a box which had held food (biscuits), and shut it up, and put it in a mule-wagon to carry it away. We asked our captain, " What would be done with them ? " Said he, " They will be carried across the sea to be looked at." Then they put back the stones upon the grave, and covered it over, and we went away. John Dunn did not stay all the time ; he showed the place, and saw them pull up the stakes, and then went on.'— Statement of a Natal Native Pioneer.

The conduct of the English in rifling Mpande's grave contrasts strangely with that of the Zulus, as described by the Correspondent of the *Times of Natal,* dating ' Umlalazi Plains, July 22, 1879.'

' I have just been talking to a man who has been to Etshowe with the Staff, and he tells me that the church and houses are all burned, pulled down, or destroyed. *The cemetery has not been interfered with in any way by the Zulus, and the whole of the monuments remain as left.*'

Will Mpande's bones be sent to England ? If so, where will they be kept—or (?) exhibited ? And by whose orders was this deed of shame committed ? Besides the infamous act of sacrilege, could a greater and more deliberate insult have been offered to the whole Zulu Nation than this ?

Note 5, page 16.

As the meeting at the Lower Tugela took place on Dec. 11, the Indunas would in fair weather have returned to the King about Dec. 16. Mr. Vijn says that, according to report, they ' had not yet come back, on Dec. 22, having very probably been detained by the rivers always overflowing their banks.'

This simple instance shows how hard and unfair it was on the part of Sir B. Frere to insist on strict punctuality on the part of the Zulu King with reference to his Ultimatum, as where he says [2222, p. 222], ' But *rigid punctuality with respect to time will be insisted on, and, unless observed, such steps as may appear necessary will be immediately taken to ensure compliance.'*

Note 6, page 16.

It was not Sihayo himself, but his brother Zuluhlenga, together with four of his sons (Mehlokazulu, Bekuzulu, Nkumbikazulu, and Tshekwana), whom Sir H. Bulwer ' requested' Cetshwayo to send down ' to be tried by the laws of this country for the serious offence they have committed in it' [2220, pp. 126, 197]. Of these four Bekuzulu was afterwards dropped out of the list, as having been with the King at the time of the raid [2260, p. 32]. Nkumbikazulu was identified among the sixteen killed by Lord Chelmsford's force on Jan. 12, the day after it had crossed over into Zululand [2242, p. 47], and nothing more has been heard about Tshekwana. But Mehlokazulu gave himself up after the Battle of Ulundi under an assumed name, with a number of others, and, being recognized, was arrested and sent down to Maritzburg, where he arrived on Sept. 4, and was lodged in the Gaol, but was subsequently examined and discharged and sent back to Zululand.

Before this act of Sihayo's sons, however, which oc-

curred towards the end of July, 1878, Sir B. Frere had
been laying his plans with a view to the Invasion of
Zululand, as appears from Comm. Sullivan's statement,
April 12, 1878 [2144, p. 32] : ' H. E. (Sir B. Frere)
pointed out to me that, as it appeared almost certain that
serious complications must shortly arise with the Zulu
Tribe of Kaffirs on the borders of Natal and the Transvaal, which *will necessitate active operations,* he considered it better that the " Active " should remain here, *in
order to render such assistance by sea and land as may
be practicable ;* ' and again he writes on Aug. 12 [2220,
p. 136] : ' The object of my visit here (Natal) . . . . *to
make myself acquainted with such points on the Coast as
might be available for co-operating with Her Majesty's
land-forces by landing troops or stores.*' It appears also
from the fact that early in July, 1878, Lord Chelmsford
made particular enquiries of a gentleman from Durban,
then in Capetown on his way to England, as to the time
of the year when he went up with Sir T. Shepstone for
the Installation of Cetshwayo in 1873, and as to whether
cannon could be taken into Zululand, and, being told that
cannon were taken up on that occasion in September, he
turned and said to one of his Staff, ' That is just the time
when we shall be in Zululand.'

This is the same gentleman, a leading member of the
Natal Bar, to whom, in June, 1878—just after the Missionaries, acting on Sir T. Shepstone's advice [2252, p.
22], had quitted Zululand, but before the raid of Sihayo's
sons had occurred—Cetshwayo sent Mr. John Dunn with
a message to this effect—' Tell Mr. —— that, in conse-

quence of various rumours and reports that have reached me from Natal, I begin to be uneasy, and afraid of getting into trouble with the English, and I wish to be advised what I am to do. I have no desire to fight, and I want all the English to know that I wish for peace. I want Mr. —— by means of the paper (*i.e.* newspaper) to make this known to all.'

At this time Mr. —— was completing his arrangements for a voyage to Europe, and was unable to give the subject that serious consideration which he would otherwise have done. He, however, desired Mr. Dunn to inform the King that, so long as he remained quiet within his own territory [which he did] he would be perfectly safe, and he (Mr. ——) and all the White colonists would see that no harm was done to him ; but, if Cetshwayo sent his men across the border to commit any depredations in British territory, then he (Mr. ——) would be one to lay down the ' paper ' and take up his gun.

Note 7, *page* 17.

There were many indications in the Blue-Books that Cetshwayo was in good faith collecting cattle in order to pay the fine, or more than the fine, demanded.

'The headman Sikonyana reported to me yesterday that the young chiefs, just down from the King's kraal, had informed him that Cetshwayo had collected 500 head of cattle ; Mnyamana and the other chiefs were to make up the number.'—Mr. Fynney, Dec. 23, 1878 [2308, p. 33].

' The cattle are still being collected, and it will be impossible now for them to be up in time '—Mr. J. Dunn, Dec. 24 [*Ib.* p. 34].

' They (two Christian Zulus) say Cetshwayo is getting the cattle together, to pay the fine demanded by the English Government. He is making Sihayo's and Mabedhla's people pay the fine between them. The latter is the headman of the Zulus who assaulted Messrs. Smith and Deighton. The King is also fining those who have been concerned in damaging the various Mission premises.' [1]—Mr. Fannin, Dec. 25, 1878 [*Ib.* p. 35].

' He (Cetshwayo) proposed at his Council that all the high chiefs and their tribes should subscribe a certain number of cattle, so as to make up a sufficient number to soften the heart of the British Government and induce it to abate its demands. The chiefs refused to give a single beast, saying that he and Sihayo had got the country into this dilemma, and that they must get out of it the best way they can. Upon this, the King has sent Mehlokazulu, Sihayo's son, to collect all the cattle belonging to his father's tribe, and bring them down to Ulundi, to see what number they can muster alone.'—Mr. Robson, Dec. 25 [*Ib.* p. 35].

' The cattle for the fine demanded by the English Government are being collected; but he (the native teacher of Bp. Schreuder at Entumeni) thinks it very doubtful if the sons of Sihayo will be given up. The King can understand a demand being made for the persons of the culprits or for a cattle fine, but not for *both*;

[1] 'The King punished the men who destroyed Kwamagwaza, by taking away all their cattle.'—C. Vijn.

they regard it like being punished twice for the same offence, or paying twice for the same article.'—Mr. Fannin, Dec. 27 [*Ib.* p. 37].

'A Zulu headman, called Tusasana, with whom I have had for some years friendly relations, sent to inform me that Cetshwayo had sent to fetch all the best of the cattle belonging to the tribe of Sihayo, and among others had taken five head from him (Tusasana). These are to be offered to the British Government.'—Mr. Robson, Dec. 27 [2242, p. 11].

' By Cetshwayo's orders Mehlokazulu is collecting the 530 cattle fine, Mabamba (? Mabedhla) 100 ; and in addition Hamu and Cetshwayo 400 head, in order to settle matters entirely.'—Mr. Fynn, Dec. 28 [2308, p. 38].

'The cattle of the tribe along the Border (Sihayo's) have been collected. It is said by Sihayo's people that cattle will be paid to the English, but the offenders will not be given up, especially Mehlokazulu, the head of Sihayo's company of the Ngobamakosi regiment, who object to give him up.' [1]—Mr. Fynn, Dec. 30 [*Ib.* p. 41].

'They will pay the fines, and more, but not give up the offenders.'—Mr. Fynn, Dec. 31 [*Ib.* p. 42].

'I was unable to get to Hamu on the second day after leaving Blood R. I was taken by an *Impi* of Cetshwayo's men near the Mhlazatshe Mountain. They had

[1] 'The King did not like to give up the two offenders ; but he would have done so had his people allowed it. The chiefs and the King's brothers, generally, wished to give them up.'—C. Vijn.

been sent to take Sihayo's cattle, and give them up to the Whitemen. They forced me to go with them : I was with them three days. They turned back, when near Rorke's Drift, on hearing that the Whitemen had already begun to take Sihayo's cattle '—referring probably to the 2,000 cattle of Sihayo captured by Col. Wood on Jan. 11 [2242, p. 45].—*Magidigidi,* Native Messenger, Jan. 12, 1879 [2252, p. 67].

But Sir B. Frere sweeps aside all such reports, and writes, Dec. 30 [2222, p. 231] :—

' He is stated to have collected cattle for the purpose; but it is useless to conjecture whether he will do more in the way of compliance than sufficient to support excuses for asking for delay.'

Note 8, *page* 19.

The Special Correspondent of the *Cape Argus* states, on the authority of Mr. John Dunn :—

'Of the other surviving sons of Panda, Hamu is the one most known outside the Nation; but he is represented as possessing all the vices of Cetshwayo, *minus* some of the more essential virtues. The favourite of the Tribe, and a man of good natural parts, is Ziwedu, whose name is but little known.'

' Nsuka, son of Sipuka, told us a bad story about Hamu's doings. When the war was ended, during the past month, Hamu, who had now returned to his country, killed by an *Impi* an old woman, and a lad, and a wife (the men ran away), and ate up the cattle of the kraal Sebeni.'

'The reason for his killing them was that, when he went over to the English, those people would not follow him, but clung to their King. So, when the war was over and he had returned from his flight, having a grudge against them, and seeing them living quietly in their kraals, he (Hamu) killed them and ate up their cattle.'— *Magema*.

Note 9, page 21.

Lord Chelmsford crossed into Zululand on Jan. 11, and rode at once to have an interview with Col. Wood, who met him (by previous arrangement) about midway between the two columns, and who writes [2242, p. 45] : ' Shortly after leaving the General on Jan. 11, I seized some cattle belonging to Nkomo and Sihayo,[1] about 2,000 ; the Zulus made only a show of resistance, stating that they were surprised. In addition to these cattle I have taken some 2,000 or 3,000 head from the Tondolosi tribe. This tribe made some show of resistance, and one Zulu was killed by Wood's Irregulars in self-defence. I am assured by the Commandant that the Zulus offered resistance to the capture of the cattle, firing on the native levies.'

Lord Chelmsford himself marched with Col. Glyn's column, and on Jan. 12 gives the return of losses inflicted on the enemy by that force since Jan. 10, as 30 killed, 4 wounded, 10 captured, together with 13 horses, 413 cattle, 332 goats, 235 sheep [*Ib.* p. 47].

[1] Probably Col. Wood captured the cattle of Sihayo, which had been collected to pay the fine (Note 7).

'On the day (Jan. 11) when Col. Glyn's column crossed the border into Zululand, cattle were grazing on the hills, men, women, and children were at their kraals, cows were being milked, as the escort [Lord Chelmsford's] passed along to meet Col. Wood's column. On that day several lots of cattle were taken from the people, and the men disarmed, with no resistance but a protest.

'On Jan. 21 six prisoners were taken by a Mounted Force under Col. ——. These were brought into Natal on Jan. 23, and on the 24th they were liberated at Rorke's Drift, but were fired upon and killed as they ran before they reached the river.'—Statement of a Natal Volunteer.

And thus the war was begun and carried on, the authors of it, as Sir B. Frere says [2242, p. 13], 'always bearing in mind that the British Government has no quarrel with the Zulu Nation!'

Note 10, *page* 31.

This was in accordance with the principle which, it is now plain, had been laid down by the Zulu King from the first, *viz.* to defend himself and not to invade Natal, as he might easily have done almost at any time, but especially after Isandhlwana, before reinforcements had arrived, and when the Colony lay, trembling and helpless, completely at his mercy. Thus Sir B. Frere writes, Feb. 12, 1879 [2269, p. 1], 'The Zulus might march at will through the country, devastating and murdering, without a chance of being checked, as long as they abstained from attacking the entrenched posts of Her Majesty's troops, which are from 50 to 100 miles apart.'

About a week after the Battle of Isandhlwana, four native wagon-drivers, who had escaped from the slaughter, stated that, just as they had crossed the Buffalo, a Zulu Induna on horseback on the other side ' shouted with a loud voice' to his men who were about to cross into Natal, ' Has he said you were to cross ? He is not invading! He is only defending the land of the Zulus! Come back!' This Induna, it appears, was Vumandaba, and his men obeyed and did not cross, whereas his colleague, Dabulamanzi, led the force which attacked Rorke's Drift. They said that themselves and Sikota (one of Cetshwayo's refugee half-brothers, a resident in Natal), and the four men with him, and also some whitemen who had got across, began first to draw breath after hearing those words of the Induna. ' We were saved by that alone ; for, if they had come across, we should just have been killed, being utterly exhausted.'

Cetshwayo's war-song, in fact, was *Uzitulele ! kaqali'muntu*, ' he keeps himself quiet ! he does not begin the attack !'=' Defence, not Defiance.' [1] Whereas Din-

---

[1] The following is another Zulu war-song, said to have been composed after the Blood River Meeting (Oct. 18, 1877), between the Zulu Indunas and Sir T. Shepstone, whom they identified at that time with the Boers, the sound of whose trousers is referred to in its last words.

Umlungu wahlab'inkosi !	The Whiteman struck at the King ! [cub !
Uzingele inkonyana yesilo !	He persecutes the Leopard's

gane's was ' *Us'eziteni ! asiyikuza sababona !* ' thou art among the enemy ! we shall never get to see them !'= ' they will all be killed before we come up'; and Chaka's was *Wagedageda izizwe ! uyauhlasela-pi na ?* ' thou hast made-an-end, made-an-end, of the tribes ! where wilt thou make a raid now ? '

But this moderation on the part of Cetshwayo was ascribed by Sir B. Frere to the ' half-heartedness ' of a savage—' I can give no reason, save the half-heartedness of a suspicious barbarian despot, to account for his not having taken advantage of the many favourable opportunities which have presented themselves in our difficulties during the last eighteen months,' Jan. 24, 1879 [1] [2252, p. 51]—and he has been spoken of repeatedly as having ' missed his opportunity !' True, he did ' miss his opportunity ' of deluging the colony with blood ; but he missed it *purposely*, having never wished to quarrel with the English, and supposing that his forbearance would have been appreciated, as it would have been by a generous foe, not bent upon his destruction at all hazards, and at the sacrifice of the right and the just.

Siyayitanda inkosi ;	We, however, love the King ;
Bangepinde bayihlabe.	They won't strike at him again,
Aingene !	Let it (the invading *Impi*)
	enter ? [liked !
Nkonyana ka'Ndaba, uy'aliwa!	Steer of Ndaba, thou art not
Ntshwayintshwayi,	Ye corduroy swishers, [again.
Ningepinde nimhlab' u Cetshwayo!	You won't strike at Cetshwayo

[1] That same evening, after writing these words, Sir B. Frere heard of the disaster at Isandhlwana on Jan. 22.

Note 11, *page* 31.

No doubt, Cetshwayo was right in his decision, according to ordinary principles of humanity. But it is not easy to see where the line is to be drawn in planning means of death for an enemy in war, when 'dynamite' has been employed in Zululand (and elsewhere in South Africa) to destroy the ignorant savage, and 'smoking out' of caves has been practised in Natal, and terrible engines, horribly destructive of human life, though requiring only skill in their use, and not any special display of valour, as Gattling-guns, shells, rockets, &c., have swept away the legs and arms and heads, or cruelly smashed the bodies, of thousands of brave, but helpless, Zulus. Thus General Pearson said at Yeovil (*Times,* Oct. 6, 1879) : 'The first time the Gattling-gun was used in war by British troops was at the Battle of Innyezane by my column on our way to Etshowe, where it did excellent service.'

But if civilised men by their secret arts may poison the *earth,* as in the following instances, why may not savages poison the *water* ?

' A trap was eventually set for them, and at the end of one of the poles a torpedo was placed, it being so arranged that the pulling up of the pole would set it off. All turned out as expected. The Zulus, with their usual coolness, when the working party had retired, went and pulled the pole up. With it a few of them disappeared skyward.'—Corresp. of *Natal Witness* with General Pearson's column, dating ' Etshowe, March 16.'

' They always followed us up in the evening when we knocked off work. We got rather sick of this; so one evening the engineers put down 18 ozs. of dynamite at the point we had left off working at, with a pole stuck in the ground and a friction tube connecting it with the dynamite. We had hardly left it when about 30 Zulus came down, saw the pole with " Torpedo " written on it, and at once tried to pull it up. It was driven down so tight that one man could not pull it out by himself; so two or three more caught hold of it, and up it came, blowing about six Zulus to atoms, and frightening the rest out of their wits.'—Corresp. of *Daily Telegraph* (*Guardian*, May 14, 1879).

This morning a strong force crossed the river under command of Colonel Russell, with the intention of drawing the Zulus from the caves where they had been secreted since our arrival. Colonel Malthus likewise accompanied the force with four companies of the 94th Regiment, who will probably surround the heights in skirmishing order, to induce the enemy to leave their caverns. If this fails, I understand that gun-cotton will be used to blast the entrances of the caves, which undoubtedly will have the desired effect. . . . .

' The troops have just returned to camp. The Engineers, under Captain Courtney, R.E., have been successful in blasting the caves.'—Correspondent of *Times of Natal* (Sept. 22, 1879), dating ' Near Lüneburg, Sept. 8.'

' Manyonyoba has fled. A few of his people having taken refuge in caves were incautiously approached by

Colonel Bray, who lost a sergeant-major and corporal of the 4th Regiment. These men, thrusting their heads through a crevice leading into a cave, were shot by the Zulus from inside. *The caves have been blown up, the people concealed in them dispersed,* and their cattle taken.' —*Times* Despatches (*Guardian*, Oct. 8, 1879).

'The attack on the caves was made by the infantry, as the ascent of the rocky mountain was impracticable to cavalry. The operations occupied several hours. After every step had been taken to compel the Zulus to surrender, and several of the troops had been shot and wounded by the enemy from the caves, *the latter were blown up with mines.*'—*Natal Mercury,* Sept. 29, 1879.

' Advices from Lüneburg, of the 8th inst., report that the " dynamite tactics " had been successfully employed against certain caves, in which some of Manyonyoba's still belligerent warriors had taken refuge.'—*Cape Argus,* Sept. 30, 1879.

'The Engineers, under Captain Courtney, were employed blasting the rocks; but I believe their efforts were fruitless, at least as far as the outcasts were concerned. For, despite the incessant shocks from the concussion of the slabs of dynamite, which were employed on the occasion, we were totally unsuccessful in driving them from their hiding-places.'—Military Correspondent of *Natal Witness,* dating ' Lüneburg, Sept. 9, 1879.'

Was the reason of this ' total' want of success ' in driving them from their hiding-places,' the very simple one that *they were all dead,* as the following extract from a private letter would seem to imply ?

After peace had been declared at Ulundi, Colonel Villiers had a brush with Manyonyoba's people who had sought refuge in a number of caves near Lüneburg.

' From one cave nine head-ringed men were induced to come out on solemn promise of their lives and fair treatment, given them by the word of Doyle, who was staff interpreter with General Wood. They came out and a few minutes afterwards they were killed [1] by Teteleku's people, who formed part of the British force.'

At another of the caves those who were inside offered effective resistance, whereupon the mouth of it was walled up, and bricks of gun-cotton (? dynamite) were thrown inside, and *blew up the cave, destroying* 400 *or* 500 *men, women and children who were in the inner recesses of the cave.* My informant, a Whiteman, said that ' there is no doubt about this, as the prisoners taken assured them that *all their women and children were inside.*'

The following occurred in the attack on Morosi's mountain (*Cape Argus*, June 17, 1879) :

' When we were on our return, Colonel Brabant, with the 1st Regiment, attacked a cave twelve miles from here—three men wounded, none seriously ; one boy accidentally shot by our own side through ball of big toe. Three days' fighting, aided by a mountain gun, made no impression. But by good luck a fissure in the rock opened right above the cave, through which dynamite and green bushes were thrown in and they were smoked

[1] ' On the same day, the natives of Russell's column, by mistake (!), killed eight of his (Manyonyoba's) men.'— Correspondent of *Natal Mercury,* Sept. 6, 1879.

out. Ten were smothered to death, and about as many more wounded, by the dynamite. The chief himself, Letsika, had a portion of his hand blown off, while trying to dip one of the cartridges in the water; *unfortunately* (!) he did not succeed, or he and some more would have been blown to atoms. Eighty odd men and 200 women and children were captured. The noise they made during the explosion was something diabolical. Drs. Hartley and Kannemeyer removed a portion of Letsika's shattered hand yesterday. Several men are suffering from inflammation of the lungs, resulting from dynamite fumes and smoke, and may yet die.'

Note 12, *page* 32.

'A remarkable incident occurred during this conversation. Hamu, who has always been looked upon as the King's brother, and for some time before the installation, as his rival, said he wished to take advantage of my presence to explain publicly what his real position in Zululand was, for, though it was well known to the Zulus, it was not known to the white inhabitants of Natal and of the Transvaal Republic. In both these countries he had been frequently accused of designing to usurp Cetshwayo's place; and, if it were not that Cetshwayo and the Zulus well knew that such a thing was impossible, these accusations would long ago have cost him his life. He then went on to explain that, though he was really Panda's son, he was legally the son of Panda's deceased brother (Nziba), and that he already possessed all the rank and property, viz. that which belonged to Nziba, which he could claim, that he had no right to claim anything which belonged to Panda's family, and that, before any such right could accrue to him, every male member of that family in Zululand and Natal (Umkungo, Sikota), and even he who is in the Transvaal (Umtonga), must die and leave no son behind. All present listened attentively to this statement, and earnestly assented to it. Cetshwayo said he wished to assure me that it was strictly true, and he was anxious that it should be known.'—Sir T. Shepstone, *Report of the Installation*, Sept. 1, 1873 [1137, p. 17].

Note 13, page 35.

Umbilini was a Swazi, 'the eldest son of Umswazi, late King of the amaSwazi' [1776, p. 52], who claimed the succession to the Swazi throne, and, being obliged to fly from Swaziland, went to *konza* (do homage) to Cetshwayo, and gave him a great deal of trouble before the war broke out, by attacking natives, Transvaal subjects, both before and after the 'Annexation,' who lived in the disputed territory north and south of the Pongolo. On the first complaint being made of his doings, Cetshwayo paid a fine for him to the Boers of 100 head of cattle; the next time he gave the Boers leave to come into his territory and kill him, and they tried to do so and failed; and then Cetshwayo himself threatened to kill him and his followers, if he offended again [1883, p. 19]. Fifteen months elapsed without any further disturbance from Umbilini. But on Oct. 12, 1878, when the King

was anxious and all Zululand agitated with fears
of the impending war, Mr. Rudolph writes [2260, p. 52]:
'The audacious Umbilini has made a daring attack on
four or five Swazi kraals,' killed four Swazi men, wounded
others, burnt the kraals, and carried off some ten women
and girls : and he adds, 'it is further reported that Umbilini about the same time also *attacked a kraal of the
Swazi subjects of Cetshwayo*, near his old cave, close to
Lüneburg, and that all the people, men, women and
children were killed, and the cattle captured and taken to
his kraals in Zululand.' But on Oct. 27, Mr. Rudolph
writes again [2222, p. 105]: 'Matters on the Swazi border
have quietly subsided. I am informed that Cetshwayo
sent to summon Umbilini to appear before him in regard
to his attack on the Swazis, and, if rumours are true, it
will go hard with Umbilini. It is stated that Cetshwayo,
at the time of Umbilini's attack on the Swazis, was in
treaty for rain with the Swazis,[1] and that he is very
angry with Umbilini because rain was refused on account
of Umbilini's deeds.

'Everything is quiet at Lüneburg, and along the Zulu
Border. The abaQulusi captains, assisted by Seketwayo,
are doing their best to find and deliver up Van Rooyen's
four cows.'

On Oct. 29, Cetshwayo's messengers state to Sir H.
Bulwer [2260, p. 58] : 'Cetshwayo also told us that
we might say that Umbilini was giving him trouble—he
had been troublesome to the Boers some months ago, and

[1] He wished to obtain rain from the common ancestors of the
Zulus and Swazis, whose graves are in Swaziland.

now had left the Zulu country with the avowed object of wresting the Swazi chieftainship from his brother, the reigning Chief—and that, if Umbilini returned to the Zulu country, he would kill him, and hoped that the Government would not disapprove of his doing so.'

And Mr. John Dunn says (Special Correspondent of the *Cape Argus*) :—' Touching Umbilini, no matter what the usage of nations may be in regard to the responsibility of rulers for the conduct of their subjects, it is an incontrovertible fact that Cetshwayo knew nothing of the raid upon the Swazis until it was all over ; and, when the report reached him, he was so incensed that he gave orders for a party to go out and kill the freebooter, pretender, or whatever he may be. This purpose of the King was frustrated through Mnyamana, the Chief Induna, who let Umbilini know what was in store for him early enough to enable him to make good his escape.'

And Sir H. Bulwer says [2260, p. 46] : ' To reassure the Settlement, Colonel Evelyn Wood sent from Utrecht a detachment of troops to Lüneburg, which had the effect of effectually stopping any further raid in that direction.'

It is apparently to these raids by Umbilini—not by the Zulus—that Colonel Buller referred in his speech at Exeter, when he said, ' It has been said that the Zulus were a brave nation, and that we invaded their country. I can only say *they were invading our territory at the beginning of the war,* and were stopped by General Wood's breaking up their column. I, as a member of that column, had to follow the track of that invasion. I can never forget my feeling. It was marked the whole way by slaughtered men, women, and children. I could not help thinking that, had we waited and had such an invasion been made in Natal, how frightful the consequences might have been.' Or he might have referred to a still more ferocious raid by the same Umbilini, assisted by Manyonyoba (also a Swazi Chief), upon the native inhabitants of the Pongolo valley, which is reported by Commandant Schermbrucker on Feb. 11, 1879 [2308, p. 65], though this took place a month after the war began, and a fortnight after the Battles of Isandhlwana and Innyezane, and hardly, therefore, ' at the beginning of the war.'

In either case, Colonel Buller, having only recently arrived, had probably no correct knowledge of the circumstances, and attributed to Cetshwayo and the Zulus the raids which Umbilini and his mongrel band of followers, chiefly of Swazi extraction, had committed on their own account upon natives who were living—not upon ' our territory,' that is, as would be supposed, upon undisputed English (*e.g.* Natal) territory, but—upon land disputed with the Transvaal Government by the Zulus or the Swazis (see below).

And, when again Colonel Buller said, ' Early in the year, before war was declared, I was riding along what was then our border, and I passed dozens of burnt-down farm-houses and deserted farms,' it must be noted that these farms lay, no doubt, within the district which on Dec. 11, 1878, Sir B. Frere declared, in accordance with the finding of the Commissioners, to belong of strict right to the Zulus, and had already so declared, if ' early

in the year, before the war was declared,' means the beginning of January, 1879, when the line in question had
ceased to be 'our border.' These farms, however, had
probably been forsaken long before, when the Border
Boers had reason to expect (from the statements of Sir T.
Shepstone) that war was meant by the English authorities
[2079, p. 139]; and the doors and windows of some of
them were certainly used as firewood by our own force—
perhaps by Colonel Buller's own men, and for his
own fire. And Sir T. Shepstone says, Nov. 23, 1877
[2000, p. 31], more than a year before Colonel Buller's
visit, 'that quite twenty farms were abandoned to the
cupidity of the Zulu soldiers on their way home'—*i.e.*
from building a kraal near Lüneburg 'as the residence of
a Zulu headman, who has received orders from the King
not to allow any molestation of the subjects of the Transvaal in the district by Zulu subjects,' Sir H. Bulwer
[2144, p. 189]—'*and that of the other native population,*'
i.e. Transvaal subjects on that border, such as formed the
native contingent attached at one time to General Wood's
column, but disbanded in consequence (it was said) of
their failure to recognise any distinction between friend
and foe, or their property, such as farmhouses, gardens,
orchards, &c. But deserted farms very soon come to
grief here in the quietest times.

Colonel Buller, it is plain, has merely re-echoed the
tone of Sir B. Frere's despatches, in which he tried to
fasten on Cetshwayo the reproach of having instigated
these raids of Umbilini, speaking of the former raid as
'a raid from Zululand,' 'regarded with no small show of

reason as the work of an advanced guard of the Zulu
Army' [2222, p. 51], and of the latter as 'made by
Umbilini with the connivance, if not under the orders,
of Cetshwayo, with the help of the *Zulu* Chief Manyonyoba,' and saying that 'the indiscriminate massacre of
every human being, armed or unarmed, including women
and children, is by no means a new feature in Zulu war-
fare' [2308, p. 62]; whereas Manyonyoba was a *Swazi*
Chief, and it is absurd to suppose that Cetshwayo sanc-
tioned this petty raid being made in contradiction to
his whole policy, and at the very time (Feb. 10, 1879)
when for months together, before the reinforcements had
arrived, he might have ravaged Natal from one end to
the other, if he had desired to do so.

But, as the Swazis were at one time called out by Sir G.
Wolesley to make a raid into Zululand (Note 28), and it is
reported that 3,000 or 5,000 Swazis are to be employed by
him in the attack on Sikukuni, it may be well to exhibit
the character of these allies of a great civilised and
Christian people, as described in the following extracts
from the Blue Books, which refer to the time when the
Swazis were called out by the Boer Government to attack
Sikukuni's captain, Johannes, who with his people were
mostly Christians :—

'*The Swazis are fiends!* One of their own men was
dying from his wounds just as they were leaving here;
so they buried him alive. He struggled and kicked off
the earth; so they tied him, and sat upon him, till he
was again buried. And two babes with their mother
were too much trouble to take with them; so they dashed

their brains out against stones before their mother's face
[1748, p. 86].

' Johannes and his men were killed by the amaSwazi,
after a brave defence. They died for what they thought
was their duty to their nation and king. Most of them
were Christians.'—Rev. A. Merensky, Aug. 18, 1876
(*Natal Mercury*).

' The Swazis (2,400) are described as having executed
their part of the programme with great bravery, unsup-
ported by the Boers, except so far as artillery was concerned. They actually carried the kraal (of Johannes)
and set fire to the huts, *ruthlessly killing the women
whom they found in them*.'—Sir H. Barkly [1748,
p. 84].

' After a few shots were fired by the cannon, the flag
was hoisted, and the Swazis went up as coolly as though
nothing was taking place, under a heavy fire from
Johannes' fortifications, stepping over those who fell, and
never breaking the order of their march till they arrived
at the forts, when with a yell they scrambled over,
assisted by their comrades' backs, and the work of death
began, lasting about half-an-hour, when all the men and
women and children were assegaid, except a few who
escaped into a cave, and three or four women they
brought out with them, Johannes' principal wife being
one.

' The endurance displayed by the Swazis was wonder-
ful. Men bleeding down their back from an assegai
stab, shot through both legs, &c., walked into town here
(Lydenburg). About thirty were killed and the same

number wounded. The noise that Friday night was terrible, and a great destruction of property took place, beams, planks, bed-planks of wagons, doors, &c., being taken to cook meal and mealies rifled from empty houses, no one daring to say much, as the Swazis were in a bad temper from the way they had been sold by the Whites, the Chief swearing he would spit in the Commandant's face and assegai him ' [*Ib.* p. 85].

' The day before yesterday the Revs. Thorne and Bawen went out to Johannes to see if they could be of service to any of the wounded, and after waiting were admitted to the kraal. But the people declined all assistance, and Johannes upbraided Mr. Thorne for allowing the English people to take part in the attack upon him, saying that he had always understood that the English were brave and noble, and did not murder women and children, nor allow it to be done, nor even countenance it by their presence, and said the attack had been made like an attack of wild beasts, and not like Christians, and that they employed the Swazis to do what they dared not do themselves, and *they had killed his women and children*' [*Ib.* p. 86].

' He (Johannes) was lying sick of the measles at the time of the battle, in the same kraal in which *his wives had been butchered by the Swazis,* and received on the occasion an assegai wound in the chest from the effects of which he eventually died.'—Sir H. Barkly [*Ib.* p. 100].

' In 1864 the Swazis accompanied the Boers against Mahali. The Boers did nothing but stand by and wit-

ness the fearful massacre. The men and *women also*
were murdered. One poor woman sat clutching her baby
eight days old ; the Swazis stabbed her through the body,
and, when she found that she could not live, she wrung
her baby's neck with her own hands to save it from
future misery' [*Ib.* p. 13].

' Neither of the cases referred to (Hottentots and
Fingos) are of the *uncontrollable ferocity* which the Swazis exhibit.'—Sir H. Barkly [*Ib.* p. 246].

' The amaSwazi have since the Sikukuni affair become impatient of restraint, and *even aggressive towards
the Transvaal.*'—Sir T. Shepstone, March 6, 1877 [1776,
p. 110].

' The amaSwazi have 10,000 men in regiments, *well
drilled and disciplined,* and their bravery can be judged
of by what a contingent furnished by them did for the
Boers during the Sikukuni war. Their experience of the
prowess of their White allies on that occasion has destroyed their respect, and made them *both defiant and
aggressive* ; and *they show signs of intending to occupy
by force lands which they consider to have been wrongfully
taken and alienated by the Republic.*'—Sir T. Shepstone,
March 12, 1877 [*Ib.* p. 127].

After reading the above, the question naturally occurs,
' Was not Cetshwayo fully justified in maintaining an
army "as well drilled and disciplined" as that of his
ferocious neighbours, the allies of the Transvaal Government, as also for the purpose of checking the constant
encroachments of that Government (the last made in
1875, for which even Sir B. Frere could find no justifica-

tion), since for sixteen years the Natal Government had trifled with his complaints, and "the replies he received seemed to him to be both temporising and evasive "?'—Sir T. Shepstone [1748, p. 24]. And then there is the further question, 'Are the Swazis to be allowed to retain their formidable military organisation, their army of " man-and-woman-slaying gladiators," whether " celibates " or not, while that of the Zulus has been broken up, and they are not permitted to have any soldiers, even for the purpose of protecting their homes from Swazi ravagers ?'

Note 14, *page* 36.

'We lost many more men at Kambula than at Isandhlwana. Our regiment, the Ngobamakosi, was so anxious to distinguish itself that we disobeyed the King's orders, and went on too fast, without waiting for our supports. When we got to the camp we were so tired that we could do nothing, and by the time our supports came up we were beaten back. Had we waited properly for our supports, we should have attacked the camp on three sides at once, and we should have taken it.'

'We encamped for the night, and then in the morning we went on to attack the Kambula Camp. When we were a long way from the camp we saw it, and it appeared as if an entrenchment had been made. When we got as near to the camp as the Victoria Bridge is from this Court-house (about half-a-mile), the White people came towards us on horseback. They commenced firing first : we did not commence there. We fired, and they fired :

I

they retired, and we followed them. That was the Ngobamakosi regiment. We thought the Zulu Army was
not far off; but it appears that at this time the main
body had not got up—I mean that portion of the Army
which subsequently rose in the rear of the Laager. The
horsemen galloped back to camp as hard as they could;
we followed and found ourselves almost close to the camp,
into which we made the greatest possible efforts to enter.
The English fired their cannon and rockets, and we were
fighting and attacking them for about the same time we
have been here to-day (about one hour)—I mean the
Ngobamakosi regiment, before the main body of the Zulu
Army came up. When it did come up, we were lying
prostrate, we were beaten, we could do no good. So
many were killed that the few who were not killed were
lying between dead bodies, so thick were the dead. The
main body of the Zulu Army attacked the camp from the
rear, and tried for a long time to get in. The Nokenke
regiment succeeded in getting into the cattle-kraal. The
Umbonambi regiment suffered much loss. Indeed the
two regiments last named were almost annihilated. It
was unfortunate for the Zulus that the Ngobamakosi
regiment should have marched quicker than was expected;
we had no intention of attacking the camp, but were
drawn on to do so by the mounted men, before the main
body of the Zulu Army came up. At Kambula the
Ngobamakosi suffered the most. At the conclusion of
the fight we were chased by the English forces over three
ridges, as far as from here to Bishopstowe (five or six
miles), and were only saved from entire destruction by

the darkness. Night came on and they left following us. Had we all come up and attacked the Kambula Camp at the same time, we should have entered the camp on that day; it is at any rate probable, if the attack had not been spoiled, as I have said. Mnyamana was the Induna in charge; Ntshingwayo also commanded under him. Cetshwayo's orders were not to attack the entrenchments, but to pass them by. If they attacked us, we were to attack them; if they remained in their Laager, then we were to pass on into the Transvaal territory, and that would bring the English forces out. But, as it happened, we found ourselves by accident in action with the English forces. Cetshwayo was very angry with us, and said we had no right to attack the Laager. He blamed and said that he would kill the officer in command [*i.e.* the commander of the Ngobamakosi], but he did not. We acted contrary to instructions at Isandhlwana, and were successful; and then we acted contrary to instructions at Kambula.' —*Mehlokazulu.*

The following facts have also been ascertained from Mehlokazulu [*Natal Witness,* Oct. 2, 1879]:—

'It must now be considered as established beyond doubt that the Zulus had no intention of making an attack that day (at Isandhlwana), because it was the day of the New Moon, on which they never transact any important business. What led on to the attack was the fact of their being themselves fired on by (as Mehlokazulu states) the Volunteers and Mounted Police, who were not supported by the Mounted Natives till they had fallen back on the first *donga* (gully).'

And so Magema was informed in Zululand :—

'Sihayo, Zibebu, and Mehlokazulu were told to go and meet the Whites at Isandhlwana, and see whether they were coming with hostile purposes or not, and Mehlokazulu was to be given up to them. When they had gone a little way forward, the Whites came into view. As they were nearly meeting them the Whites fired and struck Zibebu's horse; and so they said that the Whites were hostile. But the King had now collected many cattle to be sent to the Whites, thinking to make peace in the land. He had ordered that his men should not proceed to fight, but just sit down, and the matter be talked over and the cattle be delivered. But the Whites, as soon as they saw the Zulus, fired, and so the King's word was frustrated.'

On Jan. 22, the day of the disaster at Isandhlwana, part of Lord Chelmsford's force had a fight with the men of Matshana Mondisa, of which the following account was given by the Zulus to Magema :—

'Matshana, when he went with his force towards the General, had not the least idea that they were enemies; but, seeing some of the natives attached to the General's force, he thought it was the Zulu Army, for the Zulu Indunas had ordered him to come and join them at the rendezvous near the place where the Whitemen were. So he went on, not knowing that the enemy was there, and on foot, a little ahead of his men, his horse being led by the bridle. As they drew near, they heard the sound of the enemies' firearms. His people tried to make him go back, and they too fired, so that Matshana might have an opportunity of escaping. So he mounted and rode off, but all his force died, only Noju and another were left. They chased him a long way, but he dismounted, and ran away on foot, and escaped them.'

Lord Chelmsford, describing the movements of the force which he himself accompanied on the morning of Jan. 22, gives this account of the above affair [2252, p. 75] :—

'A general advance was then made, and the enemy retired without fighting. On the extreme right, however, the Natal Carbineers, under Captain (Theo.) Shepstone, managed to cut off about 300, who took refuge on a difficult hill, and in some caves. These were finally dislodged, with the assistance of some of the Native Contingent, and fifty were killed'—without (apparently) any loss to Captain Theo. Shepstone's force in killed or wounded.

And Colonel Crealock says [2252, p. 99] :—'During the three previous hours we had been advancing with Colonel Glyn's column against a Zulu force that fell back from hill to hill as we advanced, giving up without a shot most commanding positions.' In other words, the Zulus had no intention that day of attacking.

Lord Chelmsford goes on to describe the disaster at Isandhlwana on that same day. But the statement [p. 77]—' Lieutenant-Colonel Durnford asked Lieutenant-Colonel Pulleine to give him two companies of British Infantry, in order that he might *move up the heights on the left and attack them* (the Zulus),' and not having obtained the two companies, '*then took his* 450 *natives*

up the heights'—is misleading. For Colonel Durnford
sent a force of mounted natives (with whom went Captain George Shepstone, as one of his Staff) 'up the heights
on the left,' to ' ascertain the enemy's movements,' which,
getting sight of Zulus, fired at them, and found that
they had roused the Umcijo Regiment at the extremity
of the right wing of the Zulu Army, which was lying
quiet, having no intention of attacking, but, being fired
at, arose at once, and returned the fire, and drew on the
rest to its support.   But Colonel Durnford himself had
gone with his mounted Basutos in a different direction,
' *to the left front of the camp.*' Thus, Lieutenant Cochrane
says [p. 82] :—' Several messages were delivered, the last
one to the effect that the Zulus were retiring in all direc-
tions.   On this message, Colonel Durnford sent two
troops of mounted natives *to the top of the hills to the
left,* and took with him two troops, &c., *on to the front of
the camp,*' and ' met the enemy some four or five miles
off in great force, and, *as they showed also on our left,* we
retired in good order to the drift [? *donga* or gully] about
a quarter of a mile in front of the camp.'

Hence the statements of Captain A. Gardner [2260,
p. 81]—' I met Captain G. Shepstone, who was also
seeking Colonel Pulleine, *having a message from Colonel
Durnford, that his men were falling back, and asking
for reinforcements ;*' ' Colonel Pulleine *sent two companies to support Colonel Durnford to the hill on the
left*' [2260, p. 81]; ' I met Captain G. Shepstone, who told
me *he had been sent by Colonel Durnford for reinforcements,* that his (Colonel Durnford's) troops were heavily

engaged *to the left of our camp, beyond the hill,* and were being driven back' [2252, p. 101]; and that of Mr. Drummond, 'when, on the morning of Jan. 22, *the mounted Basutos, under the command of Colonel Durnford, R.E., discovered their position, and fired at a portion of the Umcijo Regiment,* that regiment immediately sprang up without orders and charged ; it was at once followed by the Nokenke, Mbonambi, and Ngobamakosi Regiments, the Ulundi Corps holding its ground' [p. 102]—are incorrect, as regards the clauses italicised, since Captain G. Shepstone came to ask support for *his own force* (containing Zikali's mounted men, but no 'Basutos'), and not for that far away under Colonel Durnford, saying that 'the whole Zulu Army would be upon them,' a statement which was received at first with incredulity.

Mr. Drummond, however, says [*Ib.*] : 'Colonel Durnford arrived with 250 mounted men and 250 native infantry, who were at once divided into three bodies, one being sent to the *left* [Captain G. Shepstone], who came in contact with the Umcijo Regiment, one to the *left front* [Colonel Durnford], and one to the rear.' And he adds : 'They had no intention whatever of making any attack on Jan. 22, owing to the state of the moon being unfavourable, from a superstitious point of view. The usual sprinkling of the warriors with medicine, previous to an engagement, had not taken place, nor had the war song been sung, or the religious ceremonies accompanying been performed.' In fact, Jan. 22 was the day of the New Moon, a day of abstinence or rest from serious labour, on which no business of importance

is undertaken by the Zulus; and on that day a peculiar
gloom must have been thrown over the dreadful field,
since, at half-past two, the sun was more than half
eclipsed.

But neither Lord Chelmsford, nor Colonel Crealock,
mentions the following very important fact, nor does it
appear in any official statement.

Colonel Harness, R.A., with his four guns, two companies of the 2–24th, and about fifty Natal Native Pio-
neers, on his way to a rendezvous in advance by a different route from that taken by the rest of the column,
had just halted about noon on some rising ground, when
they heard cannon-firing, and saw shells bursting against
the hills to the left of the camp, and a large body of
natives appeared in the plain below, between themselves
and the camp. Captain Church, 2–24th, with Colonel
Harness's approval, took a horse and galloped towards
them to find out who they were, when an officer rode
out to meet him saying that they were Brown's Contingent, and he was sent to say, ' Come in, every man, for
God's sake ! The camp is surrounded, and will be taken
unless helped at once!' Captain Church galloped back,
and told Colonel Harness, who was then conversing with
Major Black, 2–24th, and Major Gosset, A.D.C. Colonel
Harness said at once, ' We will march back ; ' but Major
Gosset said ' it was all bosh !' and advised him to carry
out his orders. Colonel Harness than asked Major Black
and Captain Church to give their opinions, and they both,
without hesitation, agreed with him ; whereupon, he at
once gave the order to return to the camp, and started

about 1.30, Major Gosset riding away in the direction of the General. Colonel Harness had gone over about two miles of his way to the camp, when he was overtaken by Major Gosset with an order from Lord Chelmsford to march back to the rendezvous, which order he obeyed, and the Zulus had their way in the camp undisturbed.

Again the report in the *Witness* of Mehlokazulu's statement goes on to say :—

'Speaking of the occasion of his raid into Natal, he again justified his conduct. ' *The King sent me,*' he said, ' *and I was obliged to go.* I do not see why your people should have interfered with me. *Whenever the Natal policemen came over into my country to arrest fugitives, we never hurt them, and always rather helped them.*[1] We told everyone we did not wish or intend to fight, and no damage was done to anything belonging to the British people.' This allusion to what was, I believe, a not unfrequent occurrence—the sending of Natal policemen into Zululand—is of some importance.

' With regard to the feeling of the Zulu nation, he asserts that there was a large majority in the Great Council in favour of giving him up on the first demand. Cetshwayo, however, would not hear of it, and, with considerable generosity of feeling, insisted on taking the blame on himself. " If," said the King, " I send out my

[1] According to the Special Correspondent of the *Cape Argus*, Mr. John Dunn stated, ' There formerly subsisted an arrangement by which women and cattle were both reckoned as property, and, when they crossed the river in either direction, it was customary to send them back. Latterly, as far as women were concerned, the understanding has not been carried out.'

dogs to hunt, and they do any damage, why should my dogs suffer, when I am the one to blame ? " And, acting in accordance with his expressions, he gave Sihayo's sons the opportunity to escape to Umbilini's district, where they remained till two or three days before the Battle of Isandhlwana, when they rejoined their regiment.'

No doubt, the King showed 'generosity of feeling' towards his young men,[1] by taking their fault upon himself, as he did the first fault of Umbilini (Note 13). But Mehlokazulu's assertion, 'the King sent me,' is flatly contradicted by Magema's informants of high respectability in Zululand.

'Mfunzi says that, when the messenger came to report Mehlokazulu's crossing and killing his father's wives, he was on duty, in attendance on the King. Sihayo was amazed, and so was the King, when he heard of Mehlokazulu's evil deed, and all the men present were amazed. Mehlokazulu speaks falsely. The King never ordered him to go and kill his father's wives, and his father knew nothing about that matter. That wife had run away to Natal, committing adultery with a young man. She was seen in Natal by another Zulu, who informed Mehlokazulu; for that woman jeered and said 'he was to tell Mehlokazulu to come and kill her. And so he did.' 'I talked with the Ingceku (household-officer) uMnukwa, who was always about the King. He says most posi-

---

[1] 'He is willing to risk the Zulu monarchy rather than that Sihayo's sons should be flogged, which he thinks will be the punishment given them.'—Sir H. Bulwer, Jan. 10, 1879 [2242, p. 29].

tively that Mehlokazulu speaks falsely if he says that the King told him to cross and seize and kill his father's wives. uMnukwa says that he was in attendance on Cetshwayo when the messenger came from Sihayo's kraal to report that matter, and Sihayo also was there with the King, and he too knew nothing whatever about that affair. On the arrival of the messenger the King was exceedingly surprised, and so was Sihayo surprised and shocked to hear of the evil doing of Mehlokazulu, and so were the other Indunas who were present. uMnukwa says that he now hears that Sihayo himself says that, and he is amazed to hear it. He says, however, that he sees that Sihayo himself suggested those words to Mehlokazulu, thinking that so he will escape, since they saw the King was as good as dead.'

Note 15, *page* 40.

'On April 5 Captain Prior, 80th Foot, proceeded from Lüneburg with a mounted patrol in the direction of the Upper Pongolo Drift. Having come up with twenty friendly natives, and received information that the Zulus were sweeping horses and cattle from the valley, he went in pursuit, and came within 800 yards of a few mounted men, who were hurrying on horses and cattle, which they abandoned and fled. After capturing the horses (18) and leaving them in charge, he himself went on with Private Bowen, their horses being freshest, following two Zulus who had taken the direction of Dombie (Intombe). They came eventually within 400 yards and exchanged shots with them. One of the Zulus was wounded by a bullet, and the friendly natives coming up, was assegaid. He was recognised as a younger son of Sihayo, the other, who got away, being ascertained to be Umbilini.'— *Official Notification.*

' The spy, whom they brought in captive, has given information to the effect that Umbilini had received a wound in the right breast ; but he does not say whether it is fatal to him or not.'—Corresp. of *Natal Colonist*, dating ' Kambula Hill, April 10, 1879.'

But the 'younger son of Sihayo,' who is said to have been killed on this occasion, could not have been Nkumbikazulu, as Mr. Vijn supposed, if he was 'distinctly recognised' [2242, p. 43] among those killed by Lord Chelmsford's force on Jan. 12 [Note 6].

' Only one of Sihayo's sons has died in the war ; that was not one of Sihayo's who was killed with Umbilini.'—*Magema.*

Note 16, *page* 40.

This agrees substantially with the statement made by the Zulu who was captured at the Battle of Ulundi and examined by Captain Theoph. Shepstone (Supp. to *London Gazette*, Aug. 21, 1879) :—

' The two cannon taken at Isandhlwana were at Nodwengu, but are now at the King's other kraal in the thorns (Maizekanye). No one knows how to use them. The Whiteman who writes the King's letters (C. Vijn) is a trader, who came trading at the beginning of the year,

and the King kept him, and he is always watched
[? guarded, protected], his property is not touched; he is
a lame man. *A Whiteman was made prisoner at Hlobane,
and taken to the King, who sent him back, and ordered
him to be let go near Kambula.'*

But it differs entirely from the very sensational story
reported in the *Natal Mercury*, April 26, as told by
Grandie (Grandier) himself, which says that he was
'threatened and beaten, with very little respite,' and was
sent back to Umbilini's Kafirs to be 'sacrificed to the
manes of Umbilini,' because 'some messengers came and
reported to Cetshwayo that Umbilini and his brother had
been killed in the attack on Colonel Wood's camp,' and
that he was sent back with a guard of two Zulus, who
had one gun and several assegais, and that 'on the 13th
April about noon they were resting, and, the Zulus being
sleepy, he watched his opportunity, snatched an assegai,
and pinned one man to the earth, when the other woke
up in a fright and ran for his life (!),' and Grandie then
made off, and was at last found by Mr. Rudolph's party
and brought in—which has been made the subject of a
monstrous picture in one of the London illustrated
papers. Besides the inherent improbability of this story
for one who knows what careful precautions would be
taken by Zulus sent to conduct a prisoner, white or black,
by the King's order, Grandie goes on to say that 'the
two guns captured at Isandhlwana were at the King's
kraal, but *were both spiked*,' which, though stated at the
time in one of the Natal journals, is now known to be untrue. Perhaps the above wild story may be accounted for

by the fact that, as an officer, who saw him when brought
in, has stated, he was 'quite off his head,' as he well
might have been after wandering about on the hills
without food.

But the following statements also confirm Mr. Vijn's
account.

'A short time since I had a talk with Mnyamana. On
being asked what he thought about affairs after Isandhlwana, he replied, very truly, "I went straight to Cetshwayo and advised him to make peace." He saw that,
whatever struggle they might make, it was only a matter
of time. He also contradicted the story told by Grandier.
His (Mnyamana's) version is that Cetshwayo handed
Grandier over to the Zulus to conduct him as near as
possible to the British lines, and there let him go—that
there was no intention of harming him. By a curious
coincidence one of these very guards was Klaas (who
found the Prince Imperial's uniform), and he confirms
Mnyamana's story.'—Corresp. of *Natal Mercury*, dating
'Kwamagwaza, Oct. 28, 1879.'

'What the Zulus know about Mr. Grandier is this.
He was caught at Hlobane by the force of the aba-
Qulusi, who took him to the King. When he came to
the King, he forbad that he should be harmed, gave him
two horses and an ox for slaughter on the way, and gave
him guides who should accompany him until he got out
of the dangerous places where the Zulu forces were, and
then he would travel safely till he reached his own
force.

'That force of the abaQulusi was quite one with

Umbilini. It is said that Umbilini did a very crafty thing on the top of that mountain (Hlobane). He blocked up with stones some of the entrances, so that the Whitemen would have to go together in one body. When they got to the top, seeing the mountain a nice level plain, seeing good streams of water there, but not seeing the abaQulusi, who were hiding, they said " Hlobane is a fine place ! it's like a man's head-ring ! " But the aba-Qulusi heard all that, and sprang up on all sides and stabbed them. Some of the Whitemen flung themselves into a pit of death, where there was no escape, and they were mercilessly assegaid—even two girls stabbing, one 5 Whitemen, the other 3. Mr. Grandier was seized at that time and taken to the King.'—*Magema.*

The *abaQulusi* (misspelt in various ways, *e.g. Makulusi, Bakulusini,* &c.), though under the authority of the Zulu King, were yet distinct from the Zulus, and formed a separate regiment. 'Umkabayi, daughter of Jama, of the same House (*i.e.* Mother) as Senzangakona, was the eldest of her family, and governed while Senzangakona was a minor. The kraal of the *abaQulusi* belonged to her, and that of Sebeni (Note 8) to her sister Mama. These are the daughters of Jama, father of Senzangakona, father of Chaka, Dingane, and Mpande.'—*Magema.*

Note 17, *page* 41.

' The King is at present busily engaged in erecting a Military Kraal among the hills between the Black and White Imvolosi Rivers, not far from the junction, in what he considers a very strong position, and one near to which (in his opinion) an army with cannon and baggage could not get, and consequently he is contemplating the removal of other Kraals to that locality. The large Kraal in process of erection he has named " Maizekanye," or " Let it (the enemy) come at once [once for all]."

' Cetshwayo, supported by Matshana Mondisa (his new brother-in-law), wishes to remove the Royal Kraal from near Umlambongwenya to the junction of the Imvolosi Rivers as soon as possible. But the old Zulu Councillors are against his proposal.

' Matshana Mondisa says that *in less than three years the English will have advanced over the western portion of Zululand,* and they (the Zulus) had better move before them.'—Mr. J. Shepstone, Jan. 3, 1877 [1776, p. 51].

Note 18, page 42.

This must be taken for what it is worth, as merely heard by Mr. Vijn from the Zulus.

But it would seem from the following statement that some word about making peace had reached the King from some quarter, while Col. Pearson's force was shut up at Etshowe.

' As to the coming of Dabulamanzi and Mavumengwana, they had been sent by the King—so says Lutsha, who was with the King at that time. For the Whitemen had sent to Dabulamanzi to ask for peace from the King, and Dabulamanzi went to inform the King of these words. The King sent Dabulamanzi and Mavumengwana to say that "he (the King) did not wish for war. If the Whitemen speak about peace, they ought to retire to their own land." At that time Dabulamanzi's Kraal was not yet burnt.'—*Magema.*

Note 19, *page* 46.

The following is a copy of Lord Chelmsford's Letter, transcribed from the original now in the possession of the Bishop of Natal.

' Message from Lord Chelmsford

' To Zulu King

'June 4th, 1879.

' Camp, Nondwini River.

' Your three messengers, by name Umgcwelo, Umtyibela, and Umpokotigayo, arrived this day at General Wood's Camp, where I personally heard their words, asking why war had been made—and I gather they wish to take back to the King the terms on which peace would be made.

' My answer is this :—

' 1. If Ketschwayo wishes for peace, he must give substantial proof of being in earnest.

' 2. He must, at once, restore all horses, oxen, arms, ammunition, and other property taken during the War.

' 3. One or more Regiments, to be named by me, must come under a flag of truce and, at a distance of one thousand yards from my camp, lay down their arms as a token of submission.

' 4. If this is done, I will order a cessation of hostili-

K

ties, pending discussion of final terms of peace. Until this is done, Her Majesty's armies will continue to advance.

' The next message from the King must be brought by one of his Officers who was present at the delivery of the Ultimatum in December last at the Lower Tugela. Usitwango or other well-known messenger of the King must accompany him.   ' CHELMSFORD, L.G.'

' In consequence of the representations of the messengers I modify Paragraph 2 as follows :—

'1. The oxen now at the King's Kraal, the two 7-pounder guns which are there also, to be sent in with the Ambassadors.

' 2. A promise from Ketchwayo that all the arms, &c., when collected, shall be given up.

'I will be content with one Regiment to come and lay down its arms.

' CHELMSFORD,

L.G.

' Camp on Nondwini River
'5 June, 1879.'

On the back is written :—

' This Paper to be brought back by the Ambassadors.
' J. N. CREALOCK,
A.D.G.'

As a copy of this important document must have been kept, it is difficult to see what reason there could have been for endorsing, as above, ' This Paper to be brought back by the Ambassadors,' unless indeed it was desired to keep out of sight the fact that such a preposterous demand was ever made upon the King as that in Paragraph 2, whether in its original or in its amended form, which latter required a 'promise' from Cetshwayo to do what he was utterly unable to perform, and which would therefore have only been a snare to trap him on some future occasion, because he had not fulfilled his engagement. And it was equally impossible for Cetshwayo to have compelled 'one or more Regiments'—or, as amended in the Postscript, 'one Regiment'—'to be named by Lord Chelmsford,' to come in person and 'lay down their arms.' Not even Sir G. Wolseley, after the Battle of Ulundi, has thought it necessary or expedient to insist on such demands as these in his terms of peace.

And these, be it observed, were not the 'terms of peace' laid down by Lord Chelmsford, but merely *preliminary* demands, which must be fully complied with before he would proceed to 'discussion of the final terms of peace.' But what would have been the nature of those 'final terms' may be gathered from the fact that not three weeks previously (May 16, 1879) Lord Chelmsford had written 'I consider the King should not be allowed to remain on the throne' [2374, p. 101]; nay, only two days previously (June 2, 1879) he had declared 'I would beg to say that I entirely agree in the views of Mr. Brownlee, and that no permanent peace can be counted on as long as Ketchwayo remains on the throne.' [*Ib.* p. 112].

In short it was evidently part of the unrighteous programme that no reasonable opportunity should be given to Cetshwayo for making peace with the English.

It may be noted that Lord Chelmsford says that 'the next message from the King must be brought by one of his Officers who was present at the delivery of the Ultimatum,' and that 'Sintwangu (Usitwango) or other well-known messenger of the King must accompany him'—being apparently unaware or oblivious of the fact that Sintwangu was himself present on that occasion [2222, p. 216]. In like manner Sir B. Frere says that Cetshwayo 'had not sent, in the customary form, any acknowledgment' of the Ultimatum, 'no proper acknowledgment of its receipt or any intimation, through messengers of the usual rank,' that it would be considered by the King and his Council; and again he writes [2374, p. 110] 'He might at any time send an Induna of rank, or even one of the respectable men, though not of the highest rank, who were deputed to receive the Lieut.-Governor's message at the Lower Tugela. Envoys of such standing could be sent as easily as men of doubtful position.' Whereas on Dec. 29, 1878, Sintwangu and Mpepa, who were both among the representatives of the Zulu Nation at the delivery of the Ultimatum [2222, p. 216], brought this message to the Lower Tugela, 'The King directed us to say that *he has heard the words of the Government* ; but the land is great, and *he has to put them before the Zulu Nation,* and he asks for time to do so.' This message, however, appears first in the Blue-Book of April, 1879 [2308, p. 39]; though a *later* message (Jan. 11) appears in the February Blue-Book [2242, p. 24], where three messengers state 'Cetshwayo has not yet refused to listen to the voice of Government ; but the Zulu Nation is gathered with the King at the Ondini (Ulundi) to consider those words. Cetshwayo asks the Great Chief to give him and the Zulu Nation time to send their reply,' and say that ' Sintwangu and Mpepa [misspelt Seboandu, Mpessa] are being sent with the reply of both the King and the whole Zulu Nation.'

But the word had gone forth—*Delendus est Cetshwayo!* The Invasion of Zululand, it is plain, had long been a settled thing in the minds of Sir B. Frere and Lord Chelmsford (Note 6); and considerations of fairplay and justice must give way to a crafty and, as it turned out, though not contemplated in the first instance, a ruthless and bloody, policy.

Note 20, *page* 49.

It may have been supposed that the ' White Trader,' without whose help in reading and interpreting the letter would have been useless, was actually with the King, and in that case the long delay before any reply reached the Camp may have seemed to indicate hostile intentions on the part of the King. But, in point of fact, Cetshwayo lost no time in the matter. Mr. Vijn, it appears, reached the King's Kraal on the 3rd day, that is, probably on the 6th day after the messenger started with the horses to fetch him. If, therefore, the letter, with its Postscript of June 5, reached Cetshwayo (say) on June 6, Mr. Vijn, if sent for *immediately*, might have reached the Kraal ' about 12th June, 1879,' the date he wrote upon his reply; and on June 14—he says ' as I suppose '—he writes in pencil at the King's dictation, on a leaf torn from an account-book, the following letter, copied also from the original, which was taken by the messengers to the English outposts, but (under the circumstances stated in Mr. Vijn's narrative) was carried back by them, and never reached the hands of Lord Chelmsford.

' Message from the Zulu King (Cetswayo)

' To Lord Chelmsford Esq.

'*about* 12*th of June*, 1879.

' The King has received Lord Chelmsford Esq. letter from 4th June; the matter that an answer come so late is, while I was not at the King's Kraal, he had to send up for me, far away the other side of the Black Umfolozi. I arrived here yesterday, and now in the morning he has called me to write a letter to Lord Chelmsford Esq. at Nondwini River.

' The three messengers from 4th June they are coming, and shall bring the words from the King about that letter.

' He wants me to write this letter to say, of course they must bring soon an answer back to the *whites*.

' The King says that " how can he talk with the Government? while the messengers are on the road, the armee is burning my kraals and taking my cattle; how can I forcome a fight?" He says that the armee must go backwards and leave of burning my huts and taking my cattle.

' The King wants to come here to talk with him Mr. Shepstone Esq. [Sir T. Shepstone], and Mr. J. Shepstone, and the Governor from Natal, so that all may come right again.

                     'C. VIJN for CETSWAYO.

'Sent by four messengers Unkekokin, Mapongaan, Kotjan, Umslomunvoelou [names misspelt].

'His Worship—I'm in short of paper, if you will send me some paper, ink, and pens, I will write you state of the Zulus.

            'To H.E. Lord Chelmsford Esq.

'I hope you will do one a favour to put this next small note in a envellope and send it to its place.'

The four messengers carrying the above letter appear to have reached Col. Collingwood's Camp at Fort Marshall, who sent them on to the D.A.G. at Head Quarters with the following note, dated June 22—

'I have the honor to forward 4 messengers from Cetayo who arrived this afternoon about 4 o'clock. I would not allow them to come near the fort.'

It would seem that the messengers must have been scared away from the Camp by some kind of threatening, if not by the measures, whatever they were, adopted at Fort Marshall to prevent their 'coming near the fort.' And, as Mr. Vijn's letter would seem to have been written on June 14, the question arises why they did not reach Fort Marshall before June 22. Had they (*e.g.*) been previously 'frightened' or 'detained' at some other outpost?

Note 21, *page* 50.

At Etshowe two of the King's messengers, sent to ask for terms of peace, were put in irons for six weeks, on the pretence of their being spies, and were brought down, manacled, with Lord Chelmsford's force to the Lower Tugela, after the relief of Etshowe.

And two other peace-messengers, well known and thoroughly respectable, who during the last six years had been sent repeatedly on important matters to the Natal Government, Mfunzi and Nkisimane, were first fired at on coming to the other side of the river, together with four of Bp. Schreuder's converts, dressed men, because they had not brought a white flag—of which they hardly knew the meaning at that time. They were not hit, and, a white flag of some kind having been extemporised, they were allowed to cross, when the two messengers were examined, and were afterwards bound with cords, by order of some juvenile military authority, and lay that night painfully with wrists tied behind their backs, which bonds, however, were removed next day by order of Mr. Fannin. But these messengers were also detained for more than six weeks at Kranzkop (Ntunjambili)[1] [2374, p. 111].

[1] Probably Sir M. Hicks-Beach had not been officially informed of the above facts when he stated in Parliament in reply to Mr. Richard, 'I do not know that in more than one instance his messengers have been treated with great indignity.' But he has not (apparently) informed the House that the statement, that two peace-messengers had been made prisoners and kept in irons at Etshowe for some weeks, was perfectly true, after it had been repudiated, on behalf of the Government, as 'incredible,'

Note 22, *page* 50.

The following is copied from the original letter of Lord Chelmsford :—

'From Lord Chelmsford,

'Commanding Her Majesty's Forces in South Africa.

'June 28th, 1879.

'Message to Ketchwayo.

'Your three messengers, Umgewelo, Umtyibela, and another have delivered your message, and the paper signed by C. Vijn, Trader.

'All I have to say in answer is :—

'You have not complied with all the conditions I laid down. I shall therefore continue to advance, as I told you I should. But, as you have sent me some of the cattle, and state that the two cannon are on their way, I consent not to cross the Umvolosi River' ['to-morrow,' originally, but corrected with Col. Crealock's initials] 'to-day, to give you time to fulfil the remainder of the conditions.

'Unless all my conditions are complied with by to-morrow evening, you must take the consequences.

'I return the tusks you send, to show you I shall still advance. I will keep the cattle a few days, to show I am

while Sir M. Hicks-Beach 'told the House of Commons last night (May 8) that he had heard nothing of Col. Pearson, acting on the advice of a Missionary, having put a flag of truce messenger from Cetshwayo in irons, except from statements in the press, which he did not believe.' (Plymouth Correspondent of *Cape Argus*, May 31, 1879.)

willing to make peace if you comply with the conditions laid down.

'I am willing that the men collected now at Ulundi, whom I have seen, should to the number of a Regiment (1,000) come to me and lay down their arms, as a sign of submission. They can do so at a distance from me of 500 yards and then retire; their lives are safe; the word of an English General is sufficient to ensure it.

'The arms in possession of the men around you now, taken at Sandhlwana, must be given up by them.

'Chelmsford,

'L.G.

'The four messengers sent about 20th June have never been to the General, J. N. Crealock.'

It will be seen that Lord Chelmsford still makes, as a preliminary condition for further discussion of the terms of peace, the utterly impracticable demand that Cetshwayo should compel 1,000 of his warriors to submit to the humiliation of coming in person and laying down their arms. Moreover, he hardly 'gives the King still two days more,' as Mr. Vijn says, to comply with all his conditions, but till 'to-morrow evening,' the messengers being still at his camp.

Among the three tusks sent in by the King as a token of sincerity, and rejected by Lord Chelmsford, there was one remarkably fine one, supposed to have been the fellow of that sent to the coast column, which is described as 'an enormous one in point of size, being seven feet in length, and about half a yard in circumference at the girth. It is the finest specimen of an elephant's tusk that has probably ever reached England, and must have belonged to an animal of prodigious dimensions.' This tusk was accepted by Gen. Crealock, and was sent home by Sir G. Wolseley to the Sec. of State for the Colonies— by which act, according to native usage, as well as by Lord Chelmsford's accepting the Prince Imperial's sword, we were pledged in honour and good faith, on 'the word of an English General,' to amicable relations with the King himself.

Note 23, *page* 50.

The following was the letter now written by Mr. Vijn in Cetshwayo's name to Lord Chelmsford (*Supp. to London Gazette*, Aug. 21, 1879) :—

'June 30, 1879.

'The King called me this morning to write this letter to your Worship, General Lord Chelmsford :—

'He brings with bearers a *degen*' [*i.e.* 'sword,' misprinted *dezen* in the *Gazette*, and in other papers 'dozen'!] 'as has belonged to the Prince of England (so they say, I do not know, of course) ; to-morrow morning the two 7-pounder guns and a lot of oxen will leave to-morrow morning to bring at your Worship's feet.

'For CETEWAYO,

'C. VIJN, Trader.

'Sir—P.S.—If the English army is in want for the country, please do me a favour to call for me by bearer, that I might get out of the country. I went into the country to buy cattle for blankets.

'And be your obedient servant

'C. V.

' P.S.—My really believing is, that the King wants to fight,[1] but the princes or his brothers they want peace; also the people wants to fight.

' The bearers are Mfunzi, Ukisimane [misspelt, ' Umvousie Englishman '].'

The following note was written in pencil on the envelope :—

' P.S.—Be strong, if the King send in his army, they are about 20,000.

'In haste, your obedient servant,

'C. V.'

Note 24, page 51.

'A large herd of white cattle was observed being driven from the King's Kraal towards us, but was driven back shortly afterwards.'—Lord Chelmsford, *London Gazette,* Aug. 21, 1879.

It is plain that the cannon, which were found after the battle of Ulundi, thrown aside in a *donga* (gully) between Maizekanye and Ulundi, must have been on their way down to be surrendered, as the King states, and must have been stopped at the same time as the white cattle, and by the same power, viz. the resolute will of the Zulus themselves.[2] In the Blue-Books, as far as I

[1] 'I at first was of this opinion; but afterwards, when I knew the King better, I changed my mind completely on this point.' —C. Vijn.

' Dabulamanzi may be taken to represent the Zulu Nation in his question, as he saw the King carried into captivity,— 'What has he done that he should be punished? It is not he that has been beaten, but his soldiers.'—*Cape Times (Natal Witness,* Sept. 27, 1879).

[2] 'When Lord Chelmsford called for the cattle, and guns and

have seen, no one has been generous enough to recognise this fact on behalf of the King.

In fact, Cetshwayo seems to have done all he could to show his sincerity in asking for terms of peace through more than a dozen sets of messengers. He sent in the cattle left to himself from those captured at Isandhlwana —the two cannon—his own white cattle—the splendid tusks of ivory to both columns—the Prince's sword. But no account was taken of all this. The 'tusk' and the 'sword' were coolly 'annexed'; but no spark of generous feeling was kindled in the breasts of those who had resolved to crush him. As he could not do the impossible things demanded of him before terms of peace would be even discussed, the hideous war was still carried on by Christian men in the name of England; the cry was still '*Delendus est!*'

Note 25, page 51.

On July 1 Mr. Vijn wrote another letter to Lord Chelmsford, which he may not have had an opportunity of sending, as he has forwarded what appears to be the original, from which the following is copied :—

'Sir,—I went into the Country Oct. 30, 1878, for buying Cattle. Just when my goods were sold, war commenced, and, of course, they did not spare me; they took

the two cannon, the King sent to fetch the cannon from Maize-kanye. And, as they were taking them together with the King's white cattle, a choice herd which had belonged to his father, the soldiers stopped the cattle, and the cannon were left lying there on the way; and so the army fought, and burnt the kraals, and there was an end of it.'—*Magema.*

my cattle, oxen, wagon, and guns, killed two of my servants. We went up to the King, and He refused to kill us, but took very good care for us.

'Now I must tell you what has happened yesterday (30th June, 1879). The King did send some days ago about 110 oxen back again (all the oxen which were left taken during the war, many died and many killed) to the General Lord Chelmsford. Yesterday he did send about 100 of his white oxen, but they were not crossed the White Umfolozi river yet, they were turned back by force from his soldiers named (Uncanda Inpinvu) Nkandampemvu crying for war, saying they should not be given to the Whites, when they (his men) were in alive; also they shall refuse to give the guns and ammunition taking during the war—they want to fight—but the King and his Brothers, also (Umjamman) Mnyamana, &c. they do not trust their men, because, when they once run away, they wont return again.

'I remain

'Your obed⁺ Serv⁺

'C. VIJN

'(For my life keep this secret to natives).'

Note 26, *page* 51.

This fact must be remembered when it is stated that after the Battle of Ulundi the Zulus 'forsook' their King and went to their homes. They did so, it appears, on all occasions, whether of victory or defeat. In fact, they were merely an *armed people*, not a 'standing army,' as is commonly supposed.

'They (the Zulus) say that at the time when Ulundi was burnt, the King had told his army not to fight with the Whites, if it found them stationary, since then probably they would have made a fortification, and the army would suffer badly. According to this word a large part of the Zulu force did not fight, since they saw that the Whites were stationary. They say that they went off to the King [? according to their oath—they might know where to find him, though Mr. Vijn did not]; and he ordered them to disperse, as he did not wish his people to come to an end, for they had now fought a good deal and had suffered greatly, and it did not matter if he himself was caught.'—*Magema.*

The Zulus said that, some time before the Battle of Ulundi, Cetshwayo tried to send a message to Sobantu (Bp. of Natal), to say that ' the Whitemen were pressing him hard, and he wished Sobantu to come with a carriage and take him, so that he might not come across the White Army, but give himself up in Natal, without being laid hands on.' The messengers were stopped by Bp. Schreuder, who said that 'they must not take the message, they would be blamed if they did, for he himself had been blamed because it was said that he was sending words to Sobantu' [which he never did].

Note 27, page 52.

It thus appears that Cetshwayo went away on July 3, the day before the Battle of Ulundi, and did not, with some of his brothers and chiefs, witness the battle from a neighbouring hill, as he is generally supposed to have done. The Zulu prisoner (Note 16) told Capt. Shepstone [*London Gazette*, Aug. 21, 1879], 'The Ndabakaombe was with the King, as his body-guard, at the Umlambongwenya Kraal, *from which he saw the battle.*' This man, however, said evidently what he believed, and not what he knew, since he was not in attendance on the King, as Mr. Vijn was. But the prisoner adds, in accordance with Mr. Vijn's statement—'The King said he wanted to make peace, and sent three days ago 140 of his white cattle as a peace-offering to the Great Chief leading the White Army. These cattle were turned back at the White Imvolosi at Nodwengu by the Nkandampemvu regiment, who refused to let them pass, saying they "preferred to fight" and "would not have peace." The King was then at Ulundi, and some of them were killed the day before yesterday [July 2] by the King's orders, for the army to eat. . . . We were all by order up at the Umlambongwenya Kraal the day before yesterday, when the King addressed us, and said that, as the Nkandampemvu regiment would not let the cattle go in as a peace-offering, and as we wished to fight, the White Army being now at his home, we might fight, but we were to fight the Whitemen in the open.'

Lord Chelmsford writes [*London Gazette*, Aug. 21]— 'Two messengers from Cetshwayo were seen by me about mid-day [June 30]. I have the honour of enclosing *a copy of the message sent to him, which at their request was reduced to writing* [given below]—likewise a copy of the written communication received by me through Mr. Vijn, the Whiteman with the Zulu Chief [see Note 23].

The messengers brought with them the sword of the late
Imperial Prince Louis Napoleon, which, for safe custody,
was sent back to the fort here. The messengers were
desired to take charge of the cattle which had been sent
in to me at Emtonjaneni, as I wanted to return them
now I was advancing ; but they refused to take them on
the plea of the delay it would cause in their return to
the King.'

The following is the account of the death of the
Prince and the recovery of the sword, obtained by Magema
in Zululand :—

' Mnukwa, an Innceku (household-officer) of the King
says—" We were watching as scouts, though not by the
King's orders, and were seated on a small rise, when we
saw the Whitemen coming late in the afternoon. There
was a river there, the iJojosi, and several small gullies,
at the place where we killed them. We went into a
gully, unseen by them, and crept along it, being in number about 40 or 50. When we got near to them, we
fired without their seeing us, just as they were about to
mount their horses. We fired many shots, but they all
missed. Four Whitemen had already mounted, and these
escaped ; but the other three and a dressed native had
not yet mounted. The Prince was in the act of mounting when his horse threw him, being startled at the noise
of our guns. When the horse had thrown him, it ran
away with his gun, which fell out some way off. When
he had fallen on the ground he drew a revolver and fired
twice, but missed. Xabanga, one of ours, flung an assegai
at him as he sat on the ground, and struck him in the

L

breast. Then Gwabukana came and stabbed him, and
the son of Maganga also and others. He never made the
least attempt to run away. We assegaid the other three
also, including the dressed native; we did not shoot any.
Then I took up from the ground the Prince's sword,
which had been left by our people, who were plundering
his articles of dress."[1]

'When Mfunzi and Nkisimane came back, and brought
to Cetshwayo in the evening the word of Gebuza (Mr. F.
E. Colenso) about sending in the sword, Mnukwa was at
hand, and the King obtained the sword at once from
him, and sent it in the next morning by Mfunzi and
Nkisimane. But he was afraid to say that the son of
Sobantu (the Bishop) had advised him to send it, lest the
English Authorities should be angry.'[2]

The letter of Lord Chelmsford was as follows [*London
Gazette*, Aug. 21]:—

'Camp "Amakeni"   Monday, 30th June, 1879.

'Lord Chelmsford sends following message to Ketchwayo.

[1] 'The watch, it was found, had been destroyed, so that only
the wheels remained of it; they thought that it was a case for
money, and expected to find coins inside it.'—*Magema.*

A native, sent by Col. Villiers recovered 4 guns, 1 revolver,
10 sovereigns, 10 half-crowns, 2 cartridge-belts, trousers, coat,
and waistcoat, shirt, penknife, &c.

[2] The statement in the *Cape Times* (*Natal Witness*, Sept. 30),
'Cetshwayo asserts that the first intelligence he had of the death
of the Imperial Prince was conveyed by *Lord Chelmsford's demand
for a return of the sword of his Imperial Highness*,' is wholly incorrect. Lord Chelmsford never, so far as appears, demanded
the sword, nor acknowledged the receipt of it to Cetshwayo in
any way.

' 1. If the Induna "Mundula" brings with him one (1,000) thousand Rifles taken at Sandhlwana, I will not insist on 1,000 men coming to lay them down, if the Zulus are afraid to come.

' He must bring the two cannon and the remainder of the cattle; I will then be willing to negociate.

' 2. As Ketchwayo has caused me to advance by the great delay he has made, I must now go as far as the Umvelosi River to enable my men to drink. I will consent, pending negociations, to halt on the further (Ulundi) bank of the River, and will not burn any kraals until Thursday the 3rd July—provided no opposition is made to my advance on the Umvelosi; by which day, the 3rd July, *by noon*, the conditions must be complied with.

' 3. If my force is fired upon, I shall consider negociations are at an end. And, to avoid any chance of this, it is best that Mundula come to my camp to-morrow at daybreak or to-night, and that the Zulu troops withdraw from the river and its neighbourhood to Ulundi.

' 4. I cannot stop the General with the coast army until all conditions are complied with; when they are so, I will send, as speedily as possible, a messenger to him.

' CHELMSFORD,

' Lt.-General.'

The above letter, it will be seen, contains a somewhat more reasonable demand—Lord Chelmsford here waiving the point on which he had previously insisted, viz. that a thousand Zulu warriors should submit to the personal indignity of coming in and laying down their arms—a thing which it was utterly out of the King's power to compel them to do—and requiring only that Mundula (the headman of the Nodweagu Kraal) should 'bring with him 1,000 Rifles taken at Sandhlwana,' which, notwithstanding the present temper of his men, might possibly have been carried out by the King, with the help of his brothers and councillors, or, at all events, might have been attempted.

This being the case, it is unfortunate that *this letter never reached Cetshwayo.* On being shown a copy of it, as it appeared in the *London Gazette*—the *only* letter from Lord Chelmsford to Cetshwayo which appears there —Mr. Vijn at once exclaimed ' That is not the letter Lord Chelmsford sent; that letter I never saw; it never reached the King.' As the two messengers who took in the sword, and at whose request this letter was written, were Mfunzi and Nkisimane, two thoroughly trustworthy men, it is difficult to explain the non-delivery of the letter in question, dated June 30, with which they may have started on July 1. However, it is certain that this letter—whose demands would have strongly tried his power over his people, but were not wholly beyond the bounds of possibility, as the former demands were—never reached the King, and he must not be charged with having rejected it, as when Lord Chelmsford says (*Lond. Gaz.*), ' This day (July 2) no messengers arrived from the King,' and again, ' No message has been received from Cetshwayo (July 3).'

Since the above was written the mystery has been explained by Magema bringing back from Zululand Lord

Chelmsford's letter, which Mfunzi gave him,[1] having never delivered it to the King, under the following circumstances.

'This letter from Lord Chelmsford had never been opened by anyone till it was opened by me, Magema, in Mfunzi's Kraal this 18th October, 1879.

'This letter was written to the King, to be read by the Whiteman who was there with him, and who would interpret all the words of it to the King. He (Mfunzi) and Nkisimane had set out from the King to carry that sword of the Prince with which they were sent by the Zulu King and People, and they brought back this letter from the General. When they arrived, they were told by the Indunas that "the Whiteman had gone away, and the letter was of no use now, as there was no one to read it."

'But Mfunzi says the Zulu People were hopeless and desperate in their trouble, and the hearts of the Indunas were deadened like stones, since they now saw that there was no help for them, and that the Zulu House must go to the ground. Mfunzi's words had no effect upon the Indunas, they did not listen to them at all. It seems to me, therefore, that the contents of this letter never reached the King, because the Indunas did not put faith in the words which Mfunzi brought, when he tried to explain them as well as he could, which was very imperfectly. Perhaps they deceived him purposely, or perhaps they did not and were themselves deceived, when they

[1] The copy given above has been transcribed from the original, now in the possession of the Bishop of Natal, which varies in some unimportant particulars from that given in the *London Gazette*.

said that the Whiteman had gone away, if he was still there. As to Mfunzi himself, they would not allow him to go in person to the King, in accordance with the Zulu custom, that no one must appear before the King who has just come from the enemy, being unclean.'

The fact is that Mfunzi and Nkisimane, if they started with this letter on the day when it was dated (June 30) must have reached the Zulu force in the midst of the excitement arising from the white oxen and cannon having been stopped by the Nkandampemvu when on their way to Lord Chelmsford (Note 25).

Note 28, *page* 54.

The following is a copy of the original letter of Sir G. Wolseley, which must have been either taken direct to the King by the messengers, or sent on to him by the five Chiefs addressed, and by him handed over to Mr. Vijn, as it must have been in any case, to be read and interpreted.

' Message from Sir G. Wolseley, K.C.B., G.C.M.G., &c., &c., &c., Governor of Natal and the Transvaal, and General Commanding the Forces in South Africa

' To MNYAMANE
    SEKETWAYO
    TYINGWAYO [NTSHINGWAYO]   by KWABABA
    USIBEBU [ZIBEBU]   MANYONI.
    UMQUANDI

' Sir Garnet Wolseley desires you to meet him as soon as possible at Emmangweni.   If you do not come to meet him, you will be regarded as an enemy of the English. If you do come to meet him, you will be treated as a friend and your cattle secured to you. Such cattle as you may have belonging to the King are to be sent to Sir Garnet Wolseley at Emmangweni. All the coast chiefs and Dabulamanzi the King's brother have surrendered.

' Sir Garnet Wolseley does not wish to make war with the Zulu People; he wishes on the contrary to protect them and see them happy. He wants you to go to his camp at Emmangweni to represent the people in settling the country, and looks upon you as the mouthpiece of the people under you, and is therefore anxious that you should come and see him.

' The Swazis are now collecting on the Pongolo River, and, if Sir Garnet Wolseley orders the Swazis to advance, they will soon clear out the Ngome forest. The Amatongas have sent messengers to Sir Garnet Wolseley saying they will not allow anyone to pass from Zululand through their territory.

' As you cannot now make any further resistance to the English or their Native Allies, you had better come in to Sir Garnet Wolseley before it is too late; you can help him in settling the Country, of which the English have no intention of annexing any portion.

' By command,

' CHELMSFORD,

' L.G.

' 14th July, 1879.'

Note 29, *page* 54.

In the above letter (Note 28) Sir G. Wolseley

desires Mnyamana, &c. to 'meet him,' to 'come and see him,' in which case they would be 'treated as friends' and might 'help in settling the country'—they 'had better come in to him before it is too late.' Not a word is said about bringing in their arms, and especially their guns, as a token of 'surrender.'

In point of fact the 'meeting,' which was held on July 19, was not altogether successful, since none but unwarlike coast chiefs attended, besides Dabulamanzi. Accordingly another notice was issued for a meeting on Aug. 10 at Ulundi, afterwards changed to Aug. 15 ; and Official Notices report as follows :—

' Yesterday I held satisfactory interview with the principal chiefs of the Coast District, informing them generally of plans for settlement of the country. Consider it necessary to return to Ulundi and occupy with troops, myself proceeding there. I have sent messengers to all chiefs to *meet me there* (Ulundi) about 10th of next month *to settle country*.

' Under Col. Villiers, Swazis will cross Pongolo River further north, accompanied by Macleod, political agent.' —Sir G. Wolseley, *Telegram*, July 21 (*Guardian*, Aug. 13).

' Five thousand Swazis ready to attack him (Cetshwayo)—probably will increase to 10,000, before crossing Pongolo River.'—Sir G. Wolseley, *Telegram*, Aug. 2 (*Guardian*, Aug. 27).

' Macleod reports that the Swazis have collected, and are ready to cross the Zulu frontier.

' Vice-Consul Thompson reports an interview with full Council of Amatonga Chiefs, who promise to carry out the General's wishes [by] refusing to allow Cetshwayo to take refuge in their territory.'—Chief of the Staff, Aug. 4, 1879.

' The Swazis were preparing to cross the Pongolo River on the 15th.

' Mnyamana, the Zulu Prime Minister, Ntshingwayo, these and three other important chiefs, with a large following, came in and surrendered to-day, bringing 650 head of the King's cattle. They are detained [!] until the rest of the cattle and arms are brought in. Two of the King's brothers, Sukane and Mgidhlana, also surrendered to-day.'—Do., Aug. 15.

Also the *Natal Mercury* states, Aug. 7 :—' We have been informed on excellent authority that, soon after the arrival of H.E. Sir G. Wolseley, he gave orders for 5,000 Swazis to hold themselves in readiness to cross into Zululand. He has also issued an order to be circulated amongst the Tongas, offering a reward for the capture of Cetshwayo.'

There is no doubt that the Swazis had been called out by Sir G. Wolseley's orders through Capt. Macleod, and (as Mr. Vijn says) the Zulus dreaded the onslaught of these ferocious savages upon their wives and children, with which they were threatened in the name of a Christian People. It is plain also that the Tongas did not, as Sir G. Wolseley's letter to the five chiefs would imply, ' send messengers' of their own accord to say that ' they would not allow anyone to pass out of Zululand through their territory,' but only ' promised to carry out the General's wishes' impressed upon them by Vice-Consul

Thompson. Under these circumstances it is not a little surprising that Sir M. Hicks-Beach should have spoken in Parliament as in the following extract he is stated to have done.

'Upon being asked by Mr. Anderson what truth there was in a statement that had appeared in the newspapers to the effect that certain English Officers had been deputed to stir up the Swazis and the Tongas against the Zulus, Sir M. Hicks-Beach said " the gentlemen referred to had been employed, not in stirring up the tribes mentioned against the Zulus, but in doing their best to prevent their joining the Zulus." '—*Cape Argus*, Sept. 9.

But Mr. Archibald Forbes, who was with the Head-Quarters, states as follows (*Guardian*, Aug. 6) :—

'Capt. Macleod has been commissioned to stir up the Swazis to aggression on the Zulus, stimulated by the price of 5,000 cattle placed on Cetshwayo's head. Leigh has been deputed to the Tongas, to kindle among them a mercenary friendship, and constitute them our King-catchers.'

Upon which the *Guardian* (Aug. 13) very justly remarks :—' Meantime, it is due to his (Sir G. Wolseley's) reputation that Englishmen should utterly and indignantly disbelieve the report that he has set a price on Cetshwayo's head. Observe what the case is. The man is not a rebel—not an invader—not a pretender—not a fugitive British criminal. He is a King whose authority we have recognised, and whose country we have invaded because he will not disband an army which he and his countrymen consider the foundation of their power and safety. He has not taken advantage of our unguarded state while it was unguarded. He has not even answered invasion by counter-invasion. He has merely stood gallantly on his defence.

'Even with this provocation, what should we have said of Cetshwayo if he had promised a large reward to any of our Zulu subjects who should murder Sir B. Frere or Lord Chelmsford? We should have classed it among the most disgraceful of his savage acts, worthy of the worst of barbarians.

'And yet, such is the state of mind in which some people approach a native war, that we see it stated, without an expression of surprise or horror, that a Christian Gentleman and Officer has been guilty of an act which, without these provocations, is absolutely unworthy of the worst of barbarians.'

And the following is a brief report of what was said in Parliament on this subject (*Guardian*, Aug. 20) :—

'On Thursday Mr. Anderson asked whether there was any foundation for the statement that Sir G. Wolseley had put a price on Cetshwayo's head. Sir M. Hicks-Beach replied that the statement did not appear in any communication received from South Africa.

'Mr. Anderson, thinking this reply unsatisfactory, moved the adjournment of the House, and asked whether this country was to be dragged down to a lower depth of infamy than it had already reached in connexion with this war by employing brigands and assassins to murder King Cetshwayo—a gallant King, who was carrying on a war in defence of his country. Sir M. Hicks-Beach would like to know what the Government or anyone else had said to justify the hon. member in charging Sir G. Wolseley with hiring assassins and murderers. Mr. Courtney said the right hon. gentleman seemed to mis-understand the question. The hon. member for Glasgow desired to give him an opportunity of making an indig-nant denial. But the right hon. gentleman did not deny the charge at all. Sir P. O'Brien suggested that the Government should telegraph to the Cape for information. Upon which the Chancellor of the Exchequer asked how that was to be done seeing that the Cape telegraph was not yet laid down. The subject then dropped.'

Mr. Archibald Forbes is now in England, and it does not appear that he has withdrawn the above statement as incorrect.

As Mnyamana, &c. did not bring in their arms, which was a well-known condition of ' surrender,' and accor-dingly is here insisted on, ' they are detained until the rest of the cattle and arms are brought in.' It is very plain that they did not really come in to surrender at all, in the proper sense of the word, but merely came to ' meet' or ' see' Sir G. Wolseley, induced by the specious language addressed to them, supposing that they might help, by advice or otherwise, in settling the country, but never expecting to be ' detained.'

Whether after the Battle of Ulundi Dabulamanzi ' surrendered' by bringing in his guns, does not appear. The Zulu prisoner says [*Lond. Gaz.* Aug. 21]: 'I have never heard that Dabulamanzi wanted peace or wanted to go over to the White people'—but he refers to the time before the battle. Also the Correspondent of the *Natal*

Witness, dating 'Umbalazi Plain, July 28,' says :—'The rumour is current here that Dabulamanzi wanted to escape and was shot in the leg by John Dunn.' And the *Witness* of Aug. 26 has the following—'A gentleman on Gen. Clifford's staff, who has been at Ulundi, gives us to understand that Ketshwayo's chief indunas, Mnyamana and Sigitwayo [? Ntshingwayo], who came in to discuss the terms of peace, were seized and kept prisoners in defiance of the laws of war. He also informs us that Dabulamanzi has got into disgrace, and been sent back in charge of Mr. Robertson to Kwamagwaza, because, instead of acting as a decoy for Ketshwayo, he conveyed to his chief a message, warning him that he would be sent to Robben Island if he surrendered.' [1]

The *Natal Colonist* (Aug. 28) quotes the following from the *Times of Natal* in reference to the above :—' We are requested by "a gentleman on Gen. Clifford's staff, who has been at Ulundi," to contradict the false statements contained in yesterday's *Witness*, as to Ketshwayo's chief indunas having been seized, &c. We have his authority for stating that the only bit of truth in the entire paragraph is that Dabulamanzai has been left in charge of Mr. Robertson. Every other statement which it contains is a pure fabrication.'

In spite, however, of the above contradiction, it is very clear from the facts above stated, as well as from the following extract from the report of Sir G. Wolseley's

[1] 'Dabulamanzi is now living at his kraal. But he was in great disgrace with the Whitemen because it was said that he had sent to Cetshwayo to warn him to hide himself. And, in fact, Dabulamanzi had done this.'—*Magema.*

meeting with the chiefs at Ulundi by the 'Special War Correspondent' of the *Times of Natal* (Aug. 27), present 'with Sir Garnet's Headquarters at Ulundi,' that the statement in the *Witness* is substantially true.

' After the names of the principal men had been taken down, the *durbar* was opened by John Shepstone, who asked why they had not come in before, and had brought in only cattle, leaving their guns and assegais, which they were told especially to bring. The old chief Mnyamana answered that "after the Battle of Ulundi they were so scattered that they had even now not had sufficient time to get all the cattle together. They had, however, thought it best to come in at once with what they could get, and, as they were sincere in their desire for peace, they would go back and get together all the guns, assegais, and rest of the cattle, both theirs and the King's." Upon being asked whether there were not some royal herds of white cattle to come in, they replied " No—they had all been taken away by the King, but plenty of others still remained to be brought in." The cunning old fellow then turned to Dunn, and said that he would, he knew, bear him out in the statement that the King and Nation had lost lots of oxen, &c., by lung-sickness, and that of those still remaining the greater portion were away beyond the Maizekanye direction. He was then asked whether he got the message sent to him lately about surrendering, &c., and whether that did not mention about guns and assegais especially.[1]   Several of

[1] Sir G. Wolseley's letter (Note 28) says nothing about 'guns and assegais.'

them began to talk at once, evidently apologizing [?], but mixing up the purport of every message which had been sent them since the war commenced. They were then asked "how it was another chief named 'Umvumyana' [? Mavumengwana or Vumandaba] had not come in with his guns and cattle from across the Black Imvolosi "—to which they replied that "he was coming to-morrow."

'This ended the first part of the *indaba* (business), Shepstone informing them that *the five principal chiefs would have to remain here until the guns, assegais, and rest of the cattle were brought in.* This gave rise to a lot of talk and objection, as they said that "they could not exercise their authority as well here as if they were allowed to go again, neither could they remain here, as the water was all polluted by the dead bodies of their comrades.' These objections were, however, overruled, and so the matter ended.

'After a short time, during which separate chiefs spoke, publicly and privately, to Dunn and Shepstone, the meeting broke up, the cattle were handed over to us, and all, except the five principal ones, scattered about and returned to their kraals during the afternoon, Cetshwayo's two brothers and the five hostages going into Dunn's camp and remaining with him.'

The following is the account of the matter given by Ntshingwayo, one of the five 'principal chiefs.'

'As to the going to Sir G. Wolseley of Mnyamana, Ntshingwayo, and the other Indunas, they had been sent by the King to sue for peace, bringing with them a large number of cattle, of which ten were Mnyamana's.

'I asked Ntshingwayo "You and Mnyamana, what was your object in going to the Whitemen ?" Said he, "We had been sent by the King ; we had not run away to the Whites. We had gone simply to ask for his head, that he might live and not perish. But, as we were going there, we saw the force (going out to capture the King) and were surprised.[1] A great number of (representative) Zulus went with us. When we came to the White Chiefs there, Mr. John (Shepstone) came forth and other White Chiefs, but the Governor (Sir G. Wolseley) did not appear. Mr. John asked "What's the meaning of this ? Where is the King ?" We said " We did not know ; we had left him at Ziwedu's." Said they "That son of Panda, we should not have harmed him ; we should only have admonished him." Said we "We have come to ask for his head ; for, even as to what we have been doing, I for my part should not say that we went in for war." Said he " Put here Sihayo and the King—for (said they) we think that King of yours will be hurt by you." All we desired was to place him somewhere, to live as a private person, and not as King. After that talk it was said " We now make you prisoners, you five Indunas." We begged to be allowed to go and live at another place, at Ulundi. It was refused ; but the Zulus were allowed to go away and leave us.'—*Magema*.

The Correspondent of the *Times* (apparently on the Staff of Sir Garnet Wolseley), dating 'Utrecht,

[1] They well might be surprised, since that was the day appointed for their 'meeting' Sir G. Wolseley, to talk over matters and settle the country.

Sept. 11, 1879,' writes as follows with reference to Mnyamana :—

' All the first five chiefs called up to sign the terms signed willingly, with every mark of approval, until Mnyamana's turn came. Mnyamana was formerly Prime Minister to Cetshwayo, and so firmly set are the roots of old instinctive dread and respect among the body of the Zulus that even now unusual deference is shown to Mnyamana, who in consequence assumed airs of unbecoming independence. Accordingly, when this ambitious chief found himself marked out for no especial honour, but rather signally slighted, disgust took possession of his soul. He thought the territory given to him too small for his importance, and he declined it. He said he would rather live under (Oham) Hamu. Sir Garnet told him in reply that he was by no means sorry that he should thus act—that *he was not by birth a great chief*, and that *he had been put into a high position only by Cetshwayo's favour*. Sir Garnet added he should be very glad to give Mnyamana's territory to a chief in whom he had more confidence, and *who by natural rank was more fitted to govern*. Accordingly next day the kingdom of Mnyamana was taken from him and given to another.'

The statements above italicised, with respect to Mnyamana's ' natural rank,' are wholly incorrect, and must have sounded ludicrously in the ears of the Zulus, as showing t e sublime ignorance of the Great Chief, who had come to settle the country, of the real state of things among them.

M

Mnyamana's father became under Chaka the Chief of a very large Tribe. He died a natural death, and was succeeded by the young son of his deceased elder brother, who was made by Chaka Induna of the Umbelebele Military Kraal, and so continued under Dingane. Soon after Panda came to the throne Mnyamana killed his cousin, because, he said, the Tribe had been built up by his own father, not by his uncle. He was recognized as Chief by Panda, and made by him Induna, first of Umbelebele, and then of the Tulwana Regiment, in which were enrolled under his command eight of the King's sons, including Umbulazi, Hamu, Ziwedu, Siteku, and Cetshwayo. During the whole of Panda's reign, therefore, Mnyamana was one of the most important Chiefs in Zululand—I saw him as such when I visited Panda at Nodwengu in 1859—and all that Cetshwayo did was to make him, very naturally, Chief Induna after Masipula's death in 1873.

The Correspondent of the *Natal Mercury*, dating 'near Ulundi, Oct. 18,' says—' Mnyamana, the late King's Prime Minister, is not at all satisfied, and declares that he was entirely misinterpreted in what he said about living with (Oham) Hamu.'

Note 30, *page* 55.

In point of fact Cetshwayo had not 'turned out the Missionaries;' but one of them says [2252, p. 22] ' That which moved us Missionaries chiefly, feeling it unsafe for ourselves in Zululand, was *the unsettled boundary question and the conviction that the illegality and insolence of the Zulus would compel the English Government to an armed demonstration, if not to a war with the Zulus. That which cau sedme and more other Missionaries to leave Zululand for Natal was that H.E. Sir T. Shepstone advised us to go out,* and so I went out 15th April this year (1878).'

The following extract shows the view which Missionaries themselves take of the present state of things in Zululand (*Times of Natal*, Oct. 27, 1879).

'If Sir G. Wolseley, the representative of a Christian Government, will *concede to us the same rights and privileges as we had under the now deposed heathen King,* and further, through the British Resident in Zululand, *protect our lives and property from violence, as Cetshwayo did,* we shall therewith be content :—

It is certainly a strange result of such vast expenditure and so much bloodshedding on both sides that at the present moment those Missionaries, who have most helped to bring on the late war by their denunciations of Cetshwayo to Sir B. Frere,[1] have been practically excluded

---

[1] Bishop Wilkinson, described as 'Bishop of Zululand,' and as 'having spent six years in Zululand '—though in reality, as I believe, he has spent only about three years in Zululand itself,— 'he only remained two years, and then returned home,' Letter in *Church Times*, Oct. 10, dated 'Kwamagwaza, Zululand, Aug. 14, 1879 '—and very soon abandoned his work in that country altogether, so that the administrators of the Mackenzie Memorial Fund complained (*Guardian*, Jan. 19, 1876) that he had 'left the diocese, at a critical time of its existence, without a head,'— and who is now 'living at St. Michael Carhayes Rectory, near St. Austell, Cornwall,' has also 'lifted up his heel' against Cetshwayo (*Western Morning News*), as also has the Rev. J. G. Morrow at Folkestone, described as 'a returned Missionary from

from Zululand through the action of Chief John Dunn, though, of course, the prohibition may be removed. It is known, indeed, that an Agent of the Norwegian Missionaries suggested to Sir B. Frere that such reports should be procured from the Missionaries, saying ' What you want, I suppose, is an indictment.' But it is diffi-cult to see how *any* earnest Missionary can voluntarily put himself under the rule of an *English* polygamist, whose manner of life he must necessarily condemn, directly or indirectly, in teaching his subjects, thus under-mining their loyalty and respect for their ruler, and placing himself in very awkward relations to the White Chief under whom he lives. And John Dunn's district is understood to include more than half of Zululand.

Mnyamana and Ntshingwayo, it appears, declined to

Zululand,' though when, or how long, he laboured there I am unable to say.

But they both merely re-echo the phrases of Sir B. Frere, Bp. Wilkinson speaking of 'the great man-slaying machine,' and denouncing Cetshwayo as a 'hard-hearted tyrant ' 'a treache-rous bloodthirsty savage, who has misruled his country and whose reign has been indeed a reign of terror ; there are thousands of Zulus who would be glad to escape from the wretched condition in which he keeps them,' and Mr. Morrow styling him 'an irresponsible, treacherous, and bloodthirsty despot.'

' The higher Zulus were of opinion that some of the Mis-sionaries had made their Stations places of refuge for bad characters, and that such people held themselves free from the laws of the country, which no King or Chief could allow. In a few cases I am informed the Missionaries were extremely rude to the late King, and he began to dislike to have any inter-course with them, although he had no wish to interfere with their proper mission work.'— Letter to *Natal Colonist,* Nov. 6, 1879.

be made Chiefs. ' Ntshingwayo told me that he and Mnyamana had told the Great Induna (Sir G. Wolseley) on the day when the new Chiefs were appointed in Zulu-land, that they had no wish for that new power (chief-tainship), and that they preferred to live as private indi-viduals; for their former power they had possessed on behalf of Cetshwayo, and they did not wish to hold office now on behalf the Government.'—*Magema.* The above, it is true, varies considerably from the official statement (*Guardian,* Oct. 1, 1879)—' After all the signing was finished, Mnyamana said he wished to with-draw from his district, and go and live under (Oham) Hamu. This Sir G. Wolseley allowed, it having been his first intention; only, as the old chief had given great assistance lately, he wanted to reward him in this way.'

Note 31, *page* 61.

The Rev. R. Robertson, in a letter dated ' Kwamgwaza, Nov. 4,' (*Natal Mercury,* Nov. 26, 1879) writes as follows :—

' It is a fact that the War was begun by the Imperial Government, and not by the Zulus. Further, it is also a fact, capable of the clearest proof, that not a single Mission Station was destroyed until Etshowe was occu-pied by the invading force under Col. Pearson. Then, and not till then, did the King give the order for the destruction of the Mission-buildings everywhere, his sole reason being to prevent their being made use of by the English troops, as Etshowe had been. Bp. Schreuder's Station alone escaped; but why ? The King wanted to destroy that also for the reason given; but, being at the time in communication with the Bishop, the latter successfully persuaded him to leave it standing.

'It was known before the troops entered Zululand that Etshowe was to be occupied, and Mr. Oftebro gave me the keys of the house and church, and asked me to do what I could to save his property, in particular his beautiful orchard, the pulpit, &c. I accordingly made it my business to be one of the first to enter Etshowe. With the exception of a sofa, from which the chintz covering had been rudely torn [by whom?], I found the place exactly as Mr. Oftebro had left it; the Zulus had touched nothing '—nearly nine months after Mr. Oftebro had quitted it.

In fact, some time must have elapsed, after the Station at Etshowe had been occupied (Jan. 23) and turned into a fortress by the British troops, before the Mission Stations were destroyed by the Zulus, and then not by the King's orders. Bp. Schreuder writes on March 3 as follows [2318, p. 35] :—

'The King says "Look here! I have taken care of the deserted Mission Stations, and not allowed them to be destroyed, thinking that the Missionaries in time would return to them, such as Mr. Robertson's at Kwamagwaza and Mr. Oftebro's at Etshowe. But we now see what use the Missionaries make of the Station-houses; Robertson has come with an Impi (army) to the Etshowe Mission-Station, and there is made a fort of it, the houses being turned to advantage for our enemies. Seeing this, my people have on their own account destroyed the other

Mission Stations, and, although I have not ordered this destruction, still I cannot complain of it, seeing that the houses on the Stations will serve as shelter for our present invading enemy. I am in a fix what to do with your Station (Entumeni) ; for it is reported amongst us (the report is said to originate from a man from John Dunn) that the column at Ntunjambili (Kranzkop) is to cross and march to Entumeni and turn the Station into a fort, (like) as Robertson has had the Etshowe turned into a fort. In that case I shall, much against my wish, be obliged to destroy the house at Entumeni, as a matter of self-protection—the last thing I ever thought of doing, as I have no (grudge) ill-will against you or your Station " This is the substance of the King's message to me with respect to my Station, Entumeni.'

On April 1, 1879, Mr. Fannin writes [2318, p. 65] :—

' I have had a private conversation with the recently [? on March 21, p. 60] arrived Entumeni men at Bp. Schreuder's. . . . Mr. Robertson's Station at Kwamag-waza has been utterly destroyed, the houses burnt, and the church-walls undermined and broken down. The Zulus feared it might be made a fortress of, like Etshowe. They are angry with Mr. Robertson for taking an active part in the War by accompanying the invading column. *No harm has been done to the other Mission Stations.*'

Probably these natives had not heard of the other Stations having been already destroyed, as seems to follow from Bp. Schreuder's statement. But, as Mr. Vijn heard that the King had fined those who had destroyed Kwa-magwaza, it may be that this Station was first destroyed, partly out of retaliation for Mr. Robertson's action, as well as for reasons of self-protection, and *without the King's authority*, though he appears to have allowed afterwards, though he did not order, the destruction by his people of the other Stations. Cetshwayo, however, regarded Kwamagwaza as belonging to the Bishop of Natal, to whom it was granted, for Mission purposes, by Panda in 1859.

It was of a piece with too many of our proceedings in this war that, on Oct. 6, 1878, Sir B. Frere counselled Sir H. Bulwer as follows [2220, p. 407] :—

' I would explain that the assemblages of Her Majesty's troops, of which he complains, are for protective and not aggressive purposes, and that it is the threatening attitude of his people, so little in accordance with his own language, which causes distrust.

' *I would inform him that the vessels he sees on the coast are for the most part English merchant-vessels trading to distant countries, but that the war-vessels of the English Government are quite sufficient to protect his coast from any descent by any other power.*'

Since Cetshwayo had seen on his coast for years past 'merchant-vessels trading to distant countries,' and had never been alarmed by them, Sir B. Frere must have known very well that he had made in his complaint no allusion to these, but to the war-vessels coming close in, and looking out for a place on the Zulu coast, where they might ' cooperate with Her Majesty's land-forces by landing troops or stores ' [see Note 13].

Note 32, *page* 76.

The following account of the capture of Cetshwayo is taken from a statement in the *Cape Times*, Sept. 11, 1879, from information furnished by Mr. Longcast, formerly the Rev. Mr. Robertson's wagon-driver, but described as 'a first-class Interpreter of the Head-Quarters Staff, who has lived twenty years in Zululand, and who is acquainted with every phase of life in Zululand,' and who is now stationed with Cetshwayo at the Castle, Capetown.

' We felt certain that the Zulus knew where the King was, and, if they would only give us the information, he would be caught in a few hours. *We tried threats and everything else during the hours of our bivouac, until daylight next morning, but without result.*

' That afternoon we successfully descended a very steep hill, and visited a kraal where the King had been that very morning. The chase was growing most exciting, and we immediately crossed the river Mona, and ascended a steep hill on the other side, on the crest of which was the kraal of Mbopa. Here we were thrown off the scent, and our hopes were dashed to the ground.

Having ascertained that Mbopa's son was with the King, we made Mbopa and all the people of his kraal prisoners, and carried them to the kraal of the son, which was five miles distant. . . . We [Lord Gifford and party] then returned to the rendezvous and rejoined Major Barrow. In our absence he had brought together about 40 Zulus, and we set to work to see if we could

get any information from them. For a very long
time we could not get anything out of them. *They were
as uncommunicative under the threat of being shot as
they were impenetrable to our seductive promises.* At
last, however, in the controversy one of the speakers accidentally dropped the information that one of the King's
own servants was amongst the group. He was instantly
taken aside by Major Barrow, and quietly questioned
through my interpreting. We extracted from him that
he had left the King that very morning, and *after a little
persuasion* he promised to put us on the following morning on to the King's trail; it was too late that day to do
anything further.

'At daybreak a party of us went to Mbopa's kraal
and took all the people—except the old gentleman, who
was not at home—prisoners, and, *as they would give us
no information,* which we knew they possessed, we burnt
the kraal and took the cattle. We then returned to the
main body of Lord Gifford's party, and there a *small boy*
told us that beer was constantly being carried to the King,
and that the men must know where he was. By *proper
persuasive measures* [? flogging] one Zulu was induced to
make a confession, and promised to take us to where the
King had been the day before, and where he was still.
The Kafir led us into the bush, but, as we foolishly had
not fastened him, he gave us the slip. We sent a few
shots after him, but missed him. We scoured the bush
thoroughly, but never saw King, prisoner, or anybody
else.

'*For the next two days, as the people were deceiving*

us, Major Barrow cleared the district of cattle. After the two days' cattle-lifting [1] Lord Gifford went off with his party to make another effort to capture the King. *We could get nothing from the Zulus. We were treated the*

[1] After the King had been captured and peace had been proclaimed, we still find the English Force harrying the Zulus (*Natal Mercury*, Oct. 15, 1879) :—

'Sept. 20. Col. Clarke detailed Major Barrow with all the mounted men for a two days' patrol. Here, in their supposed impregnable retreat, two chiefs had brought on themselves the weight of Sir Garnet's anger. From here had issued those raids into Natal which had so annoyed and frightened the colonists [in retaliation of repeated raids into Zululand made by Lord Chelmsford's orders]. Although now all the memory of that was nominally (!) buried under the Amnesty proclaimed by Sir Garnet, no doubt, it could not but render the Authorities little disposed to stand much nonsense from the same quarter. It was necessary to show them the contrary. Their chiefs have delayed delivering up their arms, till delay grew almost into open defiance We were sent to compel them.'

'The Chief Makando (? Manqondo) a huge, overfed, sulky-looking man, even then at first *attempted resistance.* "No, he had no guns." Then his fine (of cattle) must be paid, and accordingly he unwillingly began to pick out the very worst and mangiest starvelings in his herd. It was time to interfere, and the end of it was that we drove off every head of cattle he had. In his kraal, like almost all the villages of Zululand, we found and recaptured all sorts of trophies from Isandhlwana—sad memorials these to us. It was hard to keep our hearts quiet and our hands still. Oh! had but that stupid, sulky dog of a Kafi had but the pluck to have fired a shot or two at us [the 'attempted resistance,' therefore, did not include 'firing a shot or two '], it would have loosed us like bloodhounds from the leash—'Revenge or Death the watchword and reply.'

'Capt. Lumley rode in next. It appears he had been delayed by the Kafirs' unwillingness to deliver up their cattle, and *had been obliged to use strong measures* ' [? flogging or killing].

same at every kraal. I had been a long time in Zululand, I knew the people and their habits, and, although I believed they would be true to their King, I never expected such devotion. Nothing would move them. Neither the loss of their cattle, the fear of death, nor the offering of large bribes, would make them false to their King.

'We were returning to the place agreed upon for sleeping, much disappointed, when we suddenly met a *woman* in the bush. Being frightened out of her life by the sight of the guns and the horses, she instantly told us where the King had slept two nights previously. We took her back with us to our bivouac, and, as soon as it was dusk, we sent off a party to surround the kraal, and to bring in any men who were there as prisoners. The party went and returned with three men who were brothers.[1] They were questioned, but denied in the most solemn way that they knew anything about the King. We threatened to shoot them, but they said 'If you kill us, we shall die innocently.'[2] This was about 9 P.M., a

---

[1] It has been stated that *five* men were seized and flogged, but would not be false to their King, and that two of these escaped, and three remained, who were treated as here described.

[2] Compare Cetshwayo's words in the Thirteenth Message to the Natal Government about the disputed boundary, Nov. 11, 1875 [1748, p. 14] :—

'Cetshwayo has lately received a message from the Transvaal Government. The message was that 'all Zulus living within the boundary of the territory hitherto in dispute between the [Boer] Government and the Zulus, are to remove from that territory,' and that, 'if they do not remove upon this notice, they will be removed by force.'

'Cetshwayo desired us to urge upon the Government of Natal

beautiful moonlight night, and the picture was rather an effective one. There were all our men sitting round at their fire-places, our select tribunal facing the three men, who were calm and collected, whilst *we, as a sort of Inquisition, were trying to force them to divulge their secret. As a last resource we took one man and led him away blindfolded behind a bush, and then a rifle was fired off, to make believe that he was shot. We then separated and blindfolded the remaining two, and said to one of them ' You saw your brother blindfolded and led away. We have shot him. Now we shall shoot you. You had better tell the truth.' After a good deal of coaxing,* one told us where the King had slept the night before, and which was about 15 miles away, and also where he had seen him that very morning. We went to the other brother, and told him that we knew everything, and we got from him the same information. It was now 11 o'clock. Lord Gifford gave orders for our party to saddle up, which was smartly done, and we started off with the two brothers as guides. We left the one brother behind, so as to keep on the screw, and make the two believe he had been shot.'

And this is the ' bloodthirsty despot' of Sir B. Frere, the ' sanguinary tyrant,' the 'ruthless savage,' whom his

to interfere, to save the destruction of perhaps both countries, Zululand and Transvaal. He requests us to state that he cannot, and will not, submit to be turned out of his own home. It may be that he will be vanquished; but, *as he is not the aggressor, death will not be so hard to meet.'*

Though meant for the Boer, the above words (italicized) are singularly applicable to his war with the British.

people abhorred, whose 'history is written in characters of blood'! The Correspondent of the *Times of Natal* (Nov. 10, 1879), dating from Utrecht, Nov. 1, says 'Common belief among them (the Zulus) is that Cetshwayo will suffer capital punishment; but their sense of respect and loyalty to his name is still very strong.' Magema, from information received in Zululand, adds the following facts.

'Lutshi says that Mbopa hid the King, when he came with Zibeba to Mbopa's Kraal. The Indunas and the Zulu People knew well enough where he was hiding; but they concealed him. Mbopa's people were flogged, but yet they concealed him; and the Inncekus (King's servants) were flogged, but they did not betray him.

'When the King was in his flight making for the Ngome forest, he came to Mbopa's kraal across the Black Imvolosi. Just after he had arrived, the Whitemen came up searching for him. Mbopa went out to speak with them. They asked for the King, but Mbopa declared that he had not seen him at all. They insisted that the King was with him. Mbopa swore a great oath that he was not there, and that he did not know where he was. So they went on their way searching for him. At a kraal further on they found a man and questioned him very severely, according to their mode of flogging and threatening to kill. That man pointed out to them the Kraal of Mbopa, which they had passed. When they got back to it, they surrounded the kraal, and called Mbopa, and asked him how it was that he had deceived them. By this time Mbopa had taken the King out of his kraal, and had hidden him somewhere else. So, when they accused Mbopa of having concealed the King in his kraal, he swore again denying it, and said that they had better go into his kraal, and search for themselves in all the huts, when they would find that he was speaking the truth. And, sure enough, when the Whitemen had gone in and hunted for themselves in all the huts, they found that, after all, Mbopa was right, and that the man who directed them there must have deceived them. So they told Mbopa that he was a truth-speaker, and went on to other kraals.'

The account above given, based on the statements of Mr. Longcast, must be regarded for the present as most correct where it varies from that of the *Daily News*, which supplements the former as follows (*Guardian*, Sept. 24, 1879):—

'On Aug. 27 he (Lord Gifford) took Cetshwayo's sleeping-mat at a kraal where the King had slept. Two lads were found there, and, as they denied all knowledge of Cetshwayo's whereabouts, they were blindfolded, and a volley fired into the air. The ruse succeeded, and one, exclaiming " My brother is shot ! " promised to lead Lord Gifford to the King's retreat. Led by this boy he threaded the defiles of the forest at night, and, after a wild and perilous ride, reached at dawn of the 28th the spot, which was in an open glade. Fearing the escape of the King to the surrounding forest, Gifford sent back intelligence, and *waited till night to make the capture.* While lying hidden he watched the King slaughter an ox, and then descried a body of cavalry on the ridge opposite the kraal. This was Major Marter, who was commanding a party of dragoons. He had received Lord Gifford's intelligence, and moving down on the opposite side effected the King's capture. At 2 P.M., too sore to ride and too foot-sore to walk, Cetshwayo was brought to the camp in an ambulance cart. On the road [? eleven of] his followers tried to escape, and five were shot.'

'Escort with Cetshwayo just arrived; King walked into camp; has only 12 followers, of whom 5 are women. Dragoons captured originally 23; but Friday evening 11 tried to escape; 5 were shot, others escaped when coming through thick bush at dusk, prisoners not bound.'—Special War Correspondent of *Times of Natal*, dating 'Ulundi, Aug. 31, 1879.'

As five of the eleven, out of the King's party of twenty-three, who tried to escape in the evening dusk on the day after their capture, were shot, it is easy to see what would have been, almost to a certainty, the fate of Cetshwayo himself, if Lord Gifford had carried out his plan of making the capture at night (the hour fixed, it is said, being 8 P.M.), and if the King had made an effort to escape, as he would assuredly have done, in the evening shade and uncertain moonlight. A rifle-shot would in all probability have laid him low, and relieved Sir G. Wolseley and the Government of the difficulty of deciding how to deal with him, in the face of the English People and of all civilized and Christian men. In this case this unfortunate and noble-minded King would have perished without the chance of justice being done to him by word or act—his name blackened and his whole character and actions misrepresented through the ceaseless vituperations of Sir B. Frere, upon which were probably based the statements, unfounded in fact, of Lord Salisbury [1] and Sir Hardinge Giffard,[2] not to speak of the coarser abuse of

[1] 'Lord Salisbury, the Foreign Secretary, who ought to be among the best informed, has lately announced to you that we have been engaged in a war in South Africa, which was brought upon us in order to repel an attack by savages on our colonial dominion. That is a statement which beats all description. When it is coolly asserted by the responsible Minister of the Crown that the Zulus invaded us, we ought to be on our guard. The error is to be found in this, that not only did we invade the land of the Zulus, but unfortunately, by that terrible calamity which befel our troops, they practically drove us out of the land; they made a broad road towards the dominions of the Queen; but, having broken our bands with a heavy hand, they did not cross the little bright stream which separated their land from ours, but simply were contented to wait within their own territory for the renewal of our wanton, unprovoked, mischievous, terrible attack.'—Mr. Gladstone at Chester (*Cape Argus*, Sept. 18, 1879).

[2] 'Lord Salisbury's mendacious statement, that the late war was commenced by the Zulus invading Natal, has been capped by his colleague, Sir Hardinge Giffard, the Solicitor-General, who addressed his constituents at Launceston in the following terms:—

'Two Zulu women had taken refuge in British territory, because they would not be forced to marry men they did not like [*wholly untrue*], and had been forcibly recaptured and butchered; and for this outrage on the British flag the King declined all redress [*wholly untrue*]. When, therefore, he heard such phrases as "unjust war," "scandalous invasion of the rights of humanity," and so forth, he should like to know what constitutes an outrage which would justify one nation in demanding redress of another. The murders committed by Cetshwayo [*executions under Zulu Law*], his killing of Missionaries [*wholly untrue*], who some people apparently thought were little better than criminals, did away with the absurd

N

Lord Elcho[1]* and Sir John Astley[2]*; nor would his face, as photographed at Capetown, have given the lie to the

argument, that we were the first to cross the river. If we saw everything prepared for outrage and violence, we should naturally prevent it, if we could. This was said to be an unjust war; but Sir H. Bulwer, whom it was customary for Liberals to praise to the disadvantage of Sir B. Frere, confirmed Sir B. Frere's facts [*not all of them*].'—*Cape Argus*, Oct. 7, 1879.

In fact the seven Missionaries, who, at the suggestion of the Durban Agent of the Norwegian Missionaries, prepared for Sir B. Frere their 'indictment against Cetshwayo' [2232, p. 11, &c.], repeat, one after another, the same tale of *two* converts—not 'Missionaries'—having been killed; to whom Messrs. Oftebro and Robertson add a *third* native 'Christian,' but without mentioning, as Mr. Schmidt does [p. 20] that he was 'a *lapsed* baptized Zulu,' or, as Mr. Volker does [p. 24], that he 'had been baptized seven years ago, but was not a good Christian, and accordingly lived at the kraals more than at the Station.' One of these two converts was killed by Gaozi (one of Sir G. Wolseley's Chiefs) in consequence of Mr. Oftebro having mentioned his wish for baptism to the King without his own Chief (Gaozi)'s knowledge and against his wishes; the other had been 'smelled out' as having caused the death of certain persons by poisoning the carcase of a dead beast of which they ate, and was killed by a violent rush of their enraged friends. In neither case had the order for execution issued from Cetshwayo, though he approved of the latter *ex post facto*, as he considered that the man was guilty.

But these two were the only cases which the Missionaries could cite of native converts who had been killed—though not *as* converts—during the five years of Cetshwayo's reign. And at his accession (1873) 'the Norwegians had 9 Stations in Zululand, the Hanoverians 10, and the Church of England 3 or 4' [2220, p. 340]; while a Correspondent of the *Church Times* (Oct. 10, 1879), who dates from 'Kwamagwaza, Zululand, Aug. 14,' and had been (apparently) informed by Mr. Robertson, speaking of

---

* For Notes, see opposite page.

gross caricatures which have appeared in the English Pictorial Journals, and one of which at least has been imposed on the editor and readers of one of them as a genuine likeness of Cetshwayo.

The fact is, however, that his whole appearance and behaviour have drawn expressions of respect and admiration from British Officers, his captors, as well as from those who saw him on the road from Ulundi or have since visited him at Capetown. Thus the *Times* account says (*Guardian*, Oct. 8, 1879) :—

' Cetshwayo's personal appearance is quite unlike any of the so-called portraits, which have appeared in the pictorial press. He is an exceptionally fine specimen of the

the Church of England Mission alone, says ' Little by little this Mission has grown until 300 or 400 Christians in Zululand may be claimed as belonging to it.'

¹ ' Lord Elcho called Cetshwayo " an armed gorilla," and stated that " he flayed men alive, covered them with honey, and, while they were still alive, planted them with ants' nests "— *for which statement there is not a shadow of foundation in fact.* " A cruel and crafty gorilla " was the designation applied to Cetshwayo by Lord Elcho in the course of the discussion on Sir G. Wolseley's appointment. In the face of loud cries of " Shame ! " and " Withdraw! " the hon. member was compelled to substitute language more in accordance with the truth.'—*Cape Argus,* June 28, 1879.

² ' He (Sir John Astley) said a great many wrong-headed people thought that we never ought to have attacked the Zulu Nation. But he for one was of opinion that we could never have maintained peace unless we had done what we did. Now that we had caught " that old rascal " Cetshwayo, it behoved us to teach him better manners. If he could not learn them we must shut him up in a cage. He should very much like to have the keeping of Cetshwayo for a week.'—*Cape Argus,* Nov. 1, 1879.

noble savage, of well-proportioned and fully developed
frame, with a good-natured, broad, open face, of the prominent Zulu type. Major Poole speaks favorably of his
general amiability, and says he has given little trouble,
except on one or two occasions when he showed a sulky
disposition, and demanded to have an entire ox roasted
for his daily meal.' [1]

And the *Cape Times* says (*Natal Mercury*, Sept.
24) :—

' In spite of his immense proportions I never saw a
finer specimen of the races of South Africa or amongst
them so intelligent a face. Those who have seen the
photographs " from a painting" are made to believe that
he is monstrous in face and form—a huge carcase with a
fiendish countenance. He is nothing of the sort. His
limbs are certainly enormous, but they are still symmetri-
cal, and the great breadth of chest probably prevents
his corpulence from being hideous. The face is massive,
open, and good-natured, and lights up quickly at a pleasant thought or a humorous suggestion. There is not a
line upon the forehead or beneath the eyes to suggest he
has passed through years of deep anxiety or great excite-

---

[1] These 'one or two occasions' may have occurred at Capetown. But an officer has stated that he became 'sulky' or, rather,
his face fell, when his escort from Ulundi turned off under secret
orders to Port Durnford, instead of taking him, as he had hoped,
and as indeed had been publicly announced, to Maritzburg,—
as also that on that march he asked one day for meat, and, being
told that there was none, he asked 'Why don't you kill a
beast ? ' to which it was replied ' We have no power to do so,'
and he said ' But the cattle here are mine, and I give you leave
to kill one '—but his wish was not complied with.

ment of any kind.   He is altogether unlike Macomo,
Sandili, or Kreli.   Sandili was probably taller than he,
but never had the breadth of chest or the same fine cast
of features.   The eyes, large and lustrous, would—in the
glance I had—indicate a restless energy and quickness of
comprehension.   All those who see the King will be
astonished that one in such good condition and with so
good a face should have ever been the great war spirit of
the land.   But no unofficial person will be permitted to
see him, if the authorities can prevent it.

'He seems to think he has been harshly treated; for
(he says) he only fought and was defeated, and it is not
fair that he should be sent down with treatment very
much like that of Langalibalele, who was an insurgent,
whilst he is a King.   According to all accounts, Cetshwayo, if permitted to argue out what he is entitled to,
will be able to do so with remarkable effect.'

Note 33, page 79.

'By reason of the fighting between the Ngobamakosi
and the Tulwana regiments a quarrel arose between
Cetshwayo and Hamu, Cetshwayo blaming Hamu very
much and asking 'Why had the Ngobamakosi been
stabbed with assegais?'   For it was Hamu who had
ordered that stabbing of the Ngobamakosi, bidding the
Tulwana to stab the youngsters, Hamu being Induna of
the Tulwana and Sigcwelegcwele of the Ngobamakosi.
Hamu in his turn was very angry, saying 'Why did the
youngsters fight with the veterans?' and he went away
home in great wrath, saying that Sigcwelegcwele should

be killed before he would be appeased. And, as all Zululand sided with Hamu in this matter, Cetshwayo sent a
reprimand to Sigcwelegcwele, bidding him fly to the
forest, and the Ngobamakosi to guard him, as the Zulus
would kill him. Therefore he and the Ngobamakosi fled,
and lay hid at the Ngoye, until all who had fought had
been fined, Sigcwelegcwele himself being fined 100 head.
And so that quarrel ended and Sigcwelegcwele returned
home.'—*Statement of Mgabugabu of the Nokenke regiment.*

The Rev. Mr. Stavem, Norwegian Missionary, states
[2252, p. 19] that in this fight 'more than 100 Zulus
were killed and many more wounded.' Sir B. Frere says
(*Correspondence with the Bishop of Natal*) '*many hundred men were killed*' on this occasion. Mr. F. E. Colenso,
who was on the spot on the second Sunday after the fight,
was informed by Mr. Mullins and Mr. J. Dunn, who
helped to remove the dead, that about 50 at the outside
were killed.

Note 34, page 80.

There is good ground for believing that the number of those killed on this occasion has been enormously
exaggerated, as where Sir B. Frere speaks [2222, p. 226]
of 'the massacre of *many hundreds* of Zulu girls and
their relations, of which the sickening details will be found
in the Parliamentary Blue-Books of April, 1877 [C. 1748],
pp. 199-216,' and elsewhere speaks of 'the unparalleled
acts of barbarity committed by Cetshwayo's order in the
butchery of a number of young women' [2242, p. 17], of
'the slaughter of a *multitude* of poor unmarried girls and

women' [2260, p. 24], and again [2316, p. 18] of 'a bar-
barous massacre of a *large number* of women and girls'
and ' of his young women being *assegaid by hundreds.*'

But Mr. Osborne, Resident Magistrate of Newcastle,
who reports the matter to the Natal Government [1748,
p. 197], says '*several* girls were killed in consequence' of
their having violated the Zulu Marriage Law; and Sir
T. Shepstone in his account of the Installation in 1873
says [1137, p. 21] 'contravention of these regulations is
visited by the severest penalties.' Mr. Osborne writes
afterwards [p. 216] 'From all I have been able to learn,
Cetshwayo's conduct has been, and continues to be, disgraceful. He is putting people to death in a shameful
manner, especially girls. The dead bodies are placed by
his order in the principal paths, especially at points where
the paths intersect each other (cross-roads).[1] A *few* of
the parents of the young people so killed buried the
bodies, and thus brought Cetshwayo's wrath upon themselves, resulting not only in their own death, but destruction to the whole family.'

Government messengers report [p. 198] : 'We heard
that the King was causing *some* of the Zulus to be killed
on account of disobeying his orders'—rather, for disobeying the national 'regulations'—respecting the marriage of girls, and *we saw large numbers of cattle which
had been taken as fines.* Otherwise *the land was quiet.*
Would the land have been ' quiet' if many hundreds' of

---

[1] It was not so very long ago that in England the bodies of
criminals, who had been executed, were hung in irons on gibbets,
as a warning to others not to offend.

girls had been killed ? It is probable that in most cases the penalty was a fine of cattle, and that in the case of those killed there was some aggravation of the offence.

The Rev. Mr. Robertson says [2220, p. 345], ' I *heard* of many being killed, and a man (Lutshitshi) told me that the *Impi* to which he belonged killed no fewer than three.'

Two Zulus, seized and imprisoned as spies, but afterwards liberated, state that they *heard* that many were killed, but did not know of a single instance within their own circles of relatives, friends, and acquaintances.

Sir H. Bulwer writes as follows [1748, p. 198] :—' In the course of last month a report reached this Government that the Zulus had been putting to death *numbers of girls and young men,* who had disobeyed the King and broken the Zulu laws of marriage.

' It appears that, *according to an old custom,* the King at certain periods authorizes certain regiments to marry girls of a particular age, the girls being obliged to marry into those regiments whether they wish to do so or not; and in conformity with this custom the King, some months ago, at the Festival of Firstfruits (Umkosi), authorized the Ndhlondhlo and Dhloko regiments to marry.

' To avoid compulsory marriages with men of these regiments, various devices were resorted to by marriageable girls and by their relatives and lovers.

' The King, on the deceptions being discovered, ordered (so it was reported) *large numbers of girls and others connected with them to be killed,* and their bodies to be placed across the highroads, in order that travellers might see the King's displeasure at the laws being broken.'

Sir H. Bulwer says ' so it was reported,' but he does not say by whom. And there are no official reports in the Blue-Books which give the least intimation about ' large numbers of girls and others ' having been killed, since Mr. Osborne speaks only of ' several girls ' and ' a few of the parents,' and the messengers of ' some of the Zulus.'

Cetshwayo's reply (Nov. 2, 1876) to Sir H. Bulwer's message of remonstrance on this occasion is *the only instance* [1] on record in which he has ever failed in paying all due respect to his English ' Father,' showing plainly irritation of mind at being interfered with from without, at a difficult time, in doing what he deemed to be his duty as King. For, in ordering these executions, he was merely enforcing (as Sir H. Bulwer says) ' an old custom,' and not, as Sir B. Frere represents it, a new law laid down by himself. From his point of view the exercise of such severity was as necessary to maintaining his authority, and therefore also securing the welfare of his people, as the decimation of a mutinous regiment might appear to a General, or as the slaughter of hundreds of Langalibalele's people, hiding in caves or running away, the destruction of the tribe and plunder of all their property, and the eating up of the Putini tribe, appeared to the Natal Government necessary for maintaining its

[1] Sir B. Frere [2220, p. 26] says ' we have not a shadow excuse for doubting that he is in *his later utterances* expressing his real intention to resume the most sanguinary of his predecessors' practices '—as if there had been *many* such messages !

authority and assuring the safety and welfare of the colony in 1873. But, whatever may have been Cetshwayo's offence in respect of this message, it had been subsequently condoned by the interchange of friendly communications between himself and Sir H. Bulwer, though Sir B. Frere raked it up again from the past in support of his proceedings.

In that message,[1] however, Cetshwayo says [1748, p. 216] : ' I shall not agree to any laws or rules from Natal, *and by so doing throw the large kraal which I govern into the water.* My people will not listen unless they are killed; and, while wishing to be friends with the English, I do not agree to give my people over to be governed by laws sent to me by them.'[2] And on Jan. 1, 1878, he gives an illustration of his difficulties in his message with respect to the fight at the Umkosi (Note 57), saying [2072, p. 96]—' Cetshwayo reports to H.E. that two of his regiments have had a fight, and many of his people have been killed, at which he is much annoyed.

---

[1] ' This message was brought, not by his own men, who would have softened down any harsh expression in delivering their master's meaning, but by two Government messengers, one of whom was a Zulu refugee, living in this colony, of the party hostile to Cetshwayo.'

[2] The rest of the message was as follows [1748, p. 216] :—

' The King said in reply—" Did he ever tell Somtseu (Sir T. Shepstone) I would not kill? Did he tell the Whitepeople I made such an arrangement? Because, if he did, he has deceived them. I do kill; but I do not consider that I have done anything yet in the way of killing, Why do the Whitepeople start at nothing? I have not yet begun; I have yet to kill: it is the custom of our Nation, and I shall not depart from it.

' Why does the Governor of Natal speak to me about my

He reports this to H.E., to show that, although he warned them that he would severely punish any regiment that caused any disturbance at the Umkosi, *he cannot rule without sometimes killing them,* especially as they know that they can run to Natal.'

Mr. Mullins has stated that the number of girls killed might be set down as '*ten* at the outside.' But it now appears (Nov. 9, 1879) from information gained by Magema in Zululand, from respectable witnesses, that the number did not exceed *five* or *six,* instead of being 'many hundreds.'

' I asked Ntshingwayo how many girls were killed in 1876. He said he did not know, as he was not then in attendance on the King. But they were only a few; in his own district not a single one was killed; he had only heard of the matter by report.

laws? Do I go to Natal and dictate to him about his laws? I shall not agree, &c. [quoted above].

' Have I not asked the English to allow me to wash my spears since the death of my father Mpande (Panda) and they have kept playing with me all this time, treating me like a child? Go back and tell the English that I shall now act on my own account, and, if they wish me to agree to their laws, I shall leave and become a wanderer; but before I go it will be seen, as I shall not go without having acted.

' Go back and tell the Whitemen this, and let them hear it well. The Governor of Natal and I are equal [? *silingene,* ' we are in like positions ']: he is Governor of Natal, and I am Governor here.'

The fact is, however, that he had done nothing whatever towards 'washing his spears' according to Zulu custom, either before or after this message (Nov. 2, 1876), until the Invasion of Zululand, having neither attacked the Swazis, his old enemies, nor the encroaching Boers.

'I asked Mnukwa, the Innceku (King's household-servant) who said that "To the best of his remembrance not many girls were killed; in the case of most of the offenders cattle were eaten up. Perhaps *five* or *six* at the outside were killed, and these had done something very bad indeed, having secretly married soldiers without the King's permission, and having been passed off deceitfully as wives of elder brothers of those whom they had really married; on that account they were killed, and the kraals who did that were also punished."

'Many of the Zulus said the same. But Mfunzi and Lutsha and the son of Klaas and others said that it was not the King who killed those girls, but Hamu, Siteku, Qetuka, Mavumengwana, and certain others, who were vexed that those girls of the inNgcengce, who had long ago—it was said three years previously—been permitted by the King to marry, still refused, because they desired to marry young men, whereas those who said that they ought to be killed, said so because it was they themselves who wanted the girls for themselves as wives.'

APPENDIX.

—◦◦—

THE ZULU MILITARY SYSTEM.

The following account of the Zulu military system was furnished to the Bishop by two Zulu soldiers :—

'In Zululand a new regiment is formed as follows :—The boys, when they think themselves big enough to enlist—say from sixteen to eighteen years old—collect at the military kraals, each going to that to which his father belongs, and there they stay, milking the cows into their mouths. This is a sign that they wish to be enlisted, and when the Izinnceku (King's officers) of the military kraals see that a good many of such boys have collected, one of them reports the fact to the King, who then gives permission for the boys to be brought before him. There is no penalty for those who do not join, although, of course, they are not thought much of. Such men may marry whenever they please, and they put on the head-ring by permission of the head man of their kraal (as is the custom in Natal). If, however, a man has once enlisted, and at some future time fails to appear when his regiment is called together for any purpose, it will then be inquired, " What has become of him ?" And if he cannot give a good reason for his absence he may perhaps be killed by his regiment, but not by the King. A man who has enlisted also may not marry until the King gives leave to his regiment.

'Well, the King gives the order to collect the boys to the officer who has reported them, who delivers it to the Indunas (officers) of the different military kraals. The boys are then collected at the different military kraals, and on the appointed day messengers are sent to the King to say they are now coming. Thereupon the King has cattle killed for them, so that when they arrive they find the meat ready. The King then gives them a name, and appoints a head-ringed man as Induna over them, and either makes them into a separate regiment and orders them to build for themselves a new military kraal, or incorporates them with one of the regiments already formed, when they share the existing kraal. If, however, when the boys appear, the King thinks them too young, he may send them back to their homes to keep the cattle, till they grow bigger, as happened to the present set of boys—the Umsizi—who showed themselves to the King last year in the summer. When the boys have built their military kraal, they disperse again to their homes, for the Zulu soldiers are not kept collected together always; they just live at home with their families. Each regiment, however, has its own military kraal, presided over by two chief Indunas. It is the correct thing for the men to spend a certain time each year at their military kraal, thereby paying their respects to the King. This, however, is voluntary; the men go when they like and stay for as long or as short a time as they like. There will be usually at one kraal say from ten to twenty men at a time. This applies to the military kraals generally; at the kraal where the King is living there are usually from fifty to sixty at a time, belonging to different military kraals. The men, while in residence, are occupied in the ordinary affairs of the kraal—*e.g.* repairing the huts or cattle kraal, planting amabele (Kafir corn), &c. There are no fixed times for the calling together of the people besides the Umkosi, or Feast of Firstfruits. But the King calls them if he wants them for anything—perhaps one regiment, perhaps two, as he sees fit—either to build a new kraal or to move an old one, or for hunting parties, or to hoe his amabele crops. . . . When the time for the Umkosi draws near (about December) the King announces it, and the regiments all collect at the different military kraals for about twenty days before the appointed day, which time they spend in hoeing the King's amabele gardens in the morning, afterwards in preparing their dress, tails, feathers, &c., and in learning new dances and songs for the occasion. People learn to fight in Zululand at home, in their fathers' kraals, when they are quite little; for, when they are out herding cattle, two boys will have a quarrel and fight it out, or boys of one kraal will divide into two parties and fight with sticks, or those of one kraal will fight with those of another, and so they learn.

'The Umkosi is always held at Nodwengu, the kraal of the late King Umpande (Panda). The King walks over from Ulundi early in the morning, escorted by the Ngobamakosi regiment, which was about to be enrolled, and had been specially given to Cetshwayo by Umpande before his death. The Umkosi lasts one day only, all the regiments in turn dancing before the King. No weapons are carried at the Umkosi for fear of accidents; the men have a stick only. There are present at the Umkosi all the women of the King's household, and indeed all, or very many, of the unmarried and unencumbered women of Zululand. Anyone may go who likes, but no one would think of going with young children to such a crush. The girls in Zululand are also formed into regiments—that is to say, they just live at home and work for their fathers only; but all those of about the same age are called by one name (those now growing up are the Umtiyane, "Ensnarers"), and may not marry until the King gives leave. When he does give leave they may marry any they like, except the young men of the regiments which have not yet received permission. Sometimes the King gives permission to a regiment of young men and to a regiment of girls at the same time; but it does not follow that the young men all get wives, as the girls may prefer men of other (previously permitted) regiments, or the young men may not possess any cattle, in which case, of course, no fathers will give them their girls.'

A PROTEST AGAINST THE ZULU WAR.

The following letter was forwarded by the Aborigines' Protection Society to Sir Michael Hicks-Beach, M.P., Secretary of State for the Colonies :—

'SIR,—We desire to address you on the subject of the lamentable and disastrous war which this country is waging with the Zulus.

'In common with a large number of our fellow-countrymen, we deeply lament that the nation has been placed in the unhappy position of invading the territories, sacrificing the lives, and capturing or destroying the property of a people who have shown a desire to cultivate friendly relations with England. We also desire to remark that the national responsibility in connection with this war has been greatly increased by the unfavourable reception which, we are informed, has been given to Cetywayo's overtures of peace.

'We learn with deep regret that at public meetings lately held both in the Cape Colony and in Natal, a war policy has been enthusiastically advocated. The war is no doubt popular in the South African colonies ; but whether it would be equally so, if the colonists were required to bear the heavy and increasing burthens which it will entail, may well be doubted. We protest against a system which involves this country in the responsibility of spending its blood and treasure in a war which it has emphatically condemned.

'We earnestly hope that her Majesty's Government will seize the earliest opportunity of offering such terms of peace as the Zulu chiefs and people may reasonably be expected to accept.

'We have the honour, &c.,

(Signed) 'S. GURNEY,

'*President of the Aborigines' Protection Society.*

WESTMINSTER.

EBURY.

STANLEY of Alderley.

J. A. FROUDE.

ROBERT MOFFAT, D.D.

C. E. TREVELYAN (Bart.)

ARTHUR HOBHOUSE, K.C.S.I.

F. LEVESON GORE, M.P.

HERBERT SPENCER.

THOMAS FOWELL BUXTON (Bart.)

CHARLES J. WINGFIELD, K.C.S.I.

STOPFORD A. BROOKE.

JAMES E. ALEXANDER (Knt.), Lieutenant-General

J. E. GORST, M.P.

W. J. EASTWICK.

R. N. FOWLER, Alderman.

EDMOND FITZMAURICE, M.P.

F. A. R. RUSSELL.

CHARLES W. DILKE (Bart.), M.P.

ARTHUR E. MIDDLETON (Bart.), M.P.

J. GURNEY BARCLAY.

WILFRID LAWSON (Bart.), M.P.

HENRY FAWCETT, M.P.

LEONARD H. COURTNEY, M.P.

FREDERICK HARRISON.

JOHN RAMSAY, M.P.

J. W. PEASE, M.P.

EDMUND STURGE.

JACOB BRIGHT, M.P.

HARCOURT JOHNSTONE (Bart.), M.P.

JOSEPH COOPER.

T. A. DICKSON, M.P.

C. J. Bunyon.

H. T. Cole, Q.C., M.P.

J. Chamberlain, M.P.

John E. Erskine, Admiral.

George Palmer, M.P.

Charles Reed (Knt.).

George Howard, M.P.

Justin McCarthy, M.P.

William Fowler.

J. Lowthian Bell, M.P.

J. Westlake, Q.C.

Thomas Earp, M.P.

J. Bevan Braithwaite.

F. Pennington, M.P.

H. M. Havelock (Bart.), M.P.

Joseph Dodds, M P.

J. Humffreys Parry, Serjeant-at-Law.

A. J. Scanlon, M.P.

P. Rylands, M.P.

James Bryce, D.C.L.

J. K. Cross, M.P.

Thomas Hughes, Q.C.

A. J. Mundella, M.P.

William Shaen.

J. F. Leith, Q.C., M.P.

Robert J. Colenso.

P. A. Taylor, M.P.

R. Shaw, Major-General.

W. H. James, M.P.

C. H. Hopwood, Q.C., M.P.

Colin Mackenzie, Lieutenant-General.

Henry Richard, M.P.

Arthur Arnold.

E. T. Gourley, M.P.

Henry Crompton.

W. J. Ingram, M.P.

P. W. Bunting.

John Simon, M.P., Serjeant-at-Law.

James Heywood, F.R.S.

T. B. Potter, M.P.

Stafford Allen.

J. W. Barclay, M.P.

John Dacosta.

T. Rowley Hill, M.P.

Evans Bell.

Charles Cameron, M.P.

John Morley.

S. D. Waddy, Q.C., M.P.

Malcolm Maccoll.

Ernest Noel, M.P.

Richard Smith.

Alexander McArthur, M.P.

L. T. Cave.

Thomas Blake, M.P.

Edward Priestman.

ROBERT FERGUSON, M.P.

P. BENSON MAXWELL (Knt.).

J. C. STEVENSON, M.P.

P. W. CLAYDEN.

W. E. BRIGGS, M.P.

HENRY ALLON, D.D.

WATKIN WILLIAMS, Q.C., M.P.

THOMAS BAZLEY (Bart.), M.P.

E. S. BEESLY.

RICHARD CONGREVE.

'F. W. CHESSON,

'Secretary of the Aborigines' Protection Society.'

London: May 28, 1879.